The Cowboy Code

HOW A LADY SHOULD BE TREATED, AND HOW
TO GET YOUR MAN TO TREAT YOU
THE COWBOY WAY

Bubba Thompson
with Andrew Glassman

www.CowboyCodeUSA.com
mail@CowboyCodeUSA.com

The Cowboy Code
HOW A LADY SHOULD BE TREATED, AND HOW TO
GET YOUR MAN TO TREAT YOU THE COWBOY WAY
Bubba Thompson with Andrew Glassman

ISBN (trade paperback):   978-0-9895877-0-9
ISBN (.mobi for Kindle):   978-0-9895877-1-6
ISBN (.epub for iPad/Nook):   978-0-9895877-2-3

Printed in the United States of America.

Lead me from death to life, from falsehood to truth.

Lead me from despair to hope, from fear to trust.

Lead me from hate to love, from war to peace.

Let peace fill my heart, my world, my universe.

Amen.

Contents

FOREWORD

Maybe there's a girl—right now—that you've noticed. You think about her the moment your eyes open in the morning. You look at her just a few seconds too long every time she's around because you can't really stop. And every now and again she walks past you, or you catch a glimpse of her hair as it falls around her face, and your heart skips a beat or two. Her approval and her smile can lift you right up.

Sometimes it makes you feel more alive than anything else, and sometimes you wish it would all just go away.

You aren't sure what to do or what to say, but you are sure of one thing: *She's special, and she was sent into your life for a reason. Your mind, your body, and your higher power are telling you: "This is someone I could really love."*

Or maybe you're on the other side—you're a girl and you've been dating someone new. He's quiet and aloof, and despite the fact that he sends you all the wrong signals, you know you're hooked on him. Every time he sends you a text you try to analyze the real meaning behind his words—and all of his spelling errors don't bother you a bit. But you need more information from him and you don't know how to get it. Your mind rightly tries to protect you from getting hurt again and craves more direction, but you don't know how to get it without sounding too controlling or prying.

You aren't sure what to do or what to say, but you are sure of one thing: *He's special and was sent into your life for a reason. Your mind, your body, and your higher power are telling you: "This is someone I could really love."*

Or maybe you're one of the lucky ones: You're in a relationship with someone now and you know it's special and meant to be, but you sometimes wish you treated each other with just a little more sweetness, just a little more kindness and forgiveness. While it sounds simple, sometimes it's tough to get from here to there. You have a partner in your life whom you both like and love, but a little voice is telling you that something's missing, something that would make it just right.

These instincts are the most important instincts we have. That little voice—I want you to listen to it, and to honor it. These windows in the world, where you can really connect with another person, don't open all that often. The question is how do you handle them? How do you make the most of these opportunities to love someone?

No one has all the answers, but what I'm sharing in this book is my way of going about it. This doesn't come from a place of guaranteed success, and I'm not trying to be a know-it-all. If anything, this is a story of trying and failing, but it's also about getting right back up again.

I live by a code.

It's a code of honesty, respect, determination, and faith. And modesty.

To some people it's a little old-fashioned, and maybe a little quaint. In my opinion, America can use some more of those qualities right about now, especially in the way we treat each other.

It's a code where your word matters. Where a handshake is all it takes to seal a deal. Where you look someone in the eye and mean what you say. Where actions speak louder than words.

And mostly, it's a code where you always seek to treat others as you would hope to be treated in return.

In my part of the country, we call it the Cowboy Code.

This book is about my values, and I will try to show you how anyone can put similar values and emotions to work for them, especially in the often confusing area of love and relationships.

This is also the story of how I fell in love recently (and publicly) and the emotions that whole experience brought out in me.

My hope is that men can read it and realize there is nothing more sacred in this world than treating a lady right. And a big part of being able to do that is to find a way to open up more than usual.

My hope is that women can read it and find ways to guide their men in this direction.

My other hope is that the cowboy traditions that were instilled in me, in this culture, in this part of the world, will be carried on. There's not too many of us left.

A lot of what you are about to read is personally embarrassing. Let's just get that out there front and center!

Cowboys weren't really built to talk about their feelings and emotions, much less write about them. But in this day and age it's important. A lot of you have written to me and asked about it—about feelings and emotions—so that's why I'm sitting down and putting these thoughts together.

It's important these values are handed down. So if you're a young man coming up, or if you're raising one right now—whether you're down here in the Deep South or living in the city lights somewhere—my hope is there might be some lessons in here that will suit you—or him.

This is my story, and it's from the heart.

The Rules versus The Codes

Like I was saying, cowboys don't live by rules as much as we live by codes.

Rules are based in negativity. If you aren't following them you are "breaking rules" and are "in the wrong".

A few years ago someone tried to lay out the "rules" of getting a guy or girl to fall for you. It was a lot of stuff about waiting before you answer a text for a few hours and not going out with someone on a Friday if they didn't ask you before Tuesday or something like that.

To me, it's romantic to call someone up and say *"hi – do you wanna go grab a beer tonight I was thinking about you today?"* or tell her *"you have been on my mind I want to say hello, do you want to meet up later?"* and spontaneously ask someone out.

Who would you rather be with – someone who wants to make plans for four days from now, or the guy who wants to see you as soon as possible? OK, you want to make us wait or play hard to get – we understand that game.

What I am saying is, *all games are bad*.

Living life by saying what you feel, and acting on it -- that is a code, not a rule.

Codes are things you can aspire to, not rules that tell you what not to do, or when you should be feeling guilty because you caved in, or messed something up.

Every now and again I will put some practical advice on how the codes in the book can be acted on with some real world examples in these little boxes.

Following your heart is a code. Tricking a guy into falling for you, by giving him the false illusion that you have other plans, and are too busy to text him back is a game.

It only starts a losing game of both people playing to the others' insecurities, and that goes round and round.

This is not a guide on how to trick a guy or lure him in with foolproof methods.

These hints and ideas are ways to try to live by the code of being honest about the way you feel, and how to back up your words with actions.

1

THE ANSWER IS FAITH

On the eastern shore of Mobile Bay in Lower Alabama is one of the nicest stretches of beaches, piers, and homes you'll ever see.

On the day I arrived, you could look out over the calm blue water, the sun beating down overhead, a breeze pushing in through the tall grass, and feel like it was clear enough to see forever.

They call this area Point Clear.

A rickety old boardwalk—aged pilings and driftwood nailed together one at a time—runs down that crescent-shaped stretch of shoreline, and you can tell even through your boots that it's handmade perfection.

Every now and then someone will ride a bike past you, the tires thumping those two by fours up and down, playing a little tune, clicking and clacking the sound of a good, charming Southern life.

On one side you've got Mobile Bay: blue, vast, and calm, lapping up on a white sand beach. On the other side, you've got sprawling Southern mansions, the best in the world money can buy: wrap-around porches; ceiling fans turning from above; wide oak steps; green, white, and blue plantation shutters.

And American flags waving proudly in the air.

Sure, this place is a little above my pay grade. But a man can dream!

Today was no ordinary day. It was going to be the start of a new adventure, and I wasn't headed into any ordinary mansion.

The one I was fixing to walk into was wired with lights, cameras, and microphones. A man was reaching around my waist (watch it, pal!) and fastening one of those remote wireless transmitters to my back.

I'd signed up for a reality show about falling in love, and it was all about to begin.

The show's on CMT and it's called *Sweet Home Alabama*. A good friend of mine had recommended it and said it was fun, so I signed up, not thinking too much of it, and now suddenly …

There were people all around, talking into microphones and ear pieces like secret service agents.

Not easing my uncertainty was the fact that when a TV camera gets locked into one of those tripods, the sound it makes is identical to the buckling-metal sound my Winchester 380 makes when you slide back the firing pin. The camera people looked kind of like snipers, too, positioned along the walkway, focusing in on their targets.

One of the cameras was on a giant crane that looked like a giraffe swooping from the white picket fence to the branches of the giant oak tree in the yard. Clearly, there was nowhere to run and nowhere to hide.

My cell phone had been taken away, and my bags had been searched. I remember being pretty still, looking around, as one thought repeated in my mind:

This sure as hell ain't no place for a cowboy!

Standing there, about to walk into that mansion and start my journey on *Sweet Home Alabama*, it occurred to me that this might be the feeling a calf gets in the pen just before the gate opens and it makes its break for the far side of the arena as a galloping horse breathes down its back. I like doing the riding and the roping, but it's sure no fun being on the other end of a hooey.

It didn't matter how I was feeling, standing there. I couldn't leave. I'd given my word that I was going to go through with this, and a cowboy never goes back on his word.

You might be wondering why I did it in the first place. Why risk heartbreak and embarrassment in front of so many people?

The answer is pretty simple. It goes to the core of the way I was raised and the code by which I strive to live my life. It's the number one value in my life, as taught by my parents, my teachers, and my closest friends. It's the name I gave my company and wear on my hat and across my chest every day.

That word is *Faith*.

My name is Bubba Thompson. I grew up in a good Southern home where I was taught to treat others the way you hoped to be treated in return. In our home you said *yes sir, no sir, yes ma'am,* and *no ma'am*. But most of all, in our home faith came first.

Our home was in Orange County, Florida. Out the front window you looked up a hill at orange groves, oak trees, pasture land.

I'm proud to say my mother, Lana Thompson, is the finest woman I've ever met. Don't start me talking about my mom because it might get too mushy! But just know this—among the many important things I learned from her is how to treat a woman with respect and dignity, above all. I promised myself as a young boy that I would always strive to treat a woman right.

My Dad's name is Doug Senior. Technically, I'm Douglas Junior, but when I was a kid my older sisters called me "Bubba" and the name stuck.

I raise cattle for a living, but we ranch cowboys are a dying breed. We work a job from *can to can't*. We start when you can see the sun and we work until you can't—six or seven days a week. We go to sleep dirty and we wake up just to do it all over again.

Above all, we pride ourselves on being patriotic and humble before God.

I named my company Faith Cattle Company when I went into business for myself in my early twenties. I'd been working with a bunch of other cowboys at the time for another boss who didn't treat us well.

One evening at twilight, sitting in the arena, a couple of the cowboys and I were all talking about our dreams of a better life—a life where we struck out on our own and had only our hands and the hands of the Lord to guide our destiny. We didn't want to keep working for someone who didn't appreciate the long hours and the blood and sweat we were putting into the job.

Leaving was a big decision, and it scared the living daylights out of all of us, that's for sure. How do you walk away from a steady, decent wage, and risk it all on your own shoulders?

We got together, my partners and I, and decided if we didn't take the risk, we'd never know if we had the goods to make it on our own terms. So we all shook on it. We were going out on faith alone, and then and there our company was born.

Today we move about 14,000 cattle a year, and we tend to more than 400 acres in the small town of Geneva, Alabama, plus some on the outskirts of Florida.

Through it all, I've found that the word *faith*—thinking of it, talking about it, and living it—has kept me joyful, appreciative, and humble.

If I believe that God truly has a plan for me, then this experiment with national television must have been a part of it! This opportunity, strange as it was, must have been in front of me for a reason.

So I pulled down my hat, and when the man with the earpiece told me it was my turn, I walked down that rickety, sand-covered boardwalk and into that old mansion.

The giant crane swung low across the grass as I came through the white picket gate, but I knew these cameras and the microphones weren't going to get to me. I had faith that this was all going to work out okay.

And it has, even though most of you know that after just about four weeks in that house, I walked away brokenhearted.

I mean to tell you I was really stung in the chest from it. I had a vision of my life going forward with a woman I had fallen deeply in love with. I bought her a ring and was ready to make the ultimate commitment.

But I don't look back at the experience with any regret at all. I went into each and every day determined to be positive and to express the emotions I was truly feeling. A funny thing happens when you put down the cell phone, get away from the television, and put your day-to-day worries off to the side: You start to feel things and form relationships with the people around you. It forces you to concentrate on your fellow man and to reach down inside yourself.

I think these are good things. I think America could use a bit more fellowship and understanding.

Inside me, I was feeling things I'd never felt before. There was a wonderful woman who represented many of the ideals I'm searching for—kindness, sweetness, sincerity, great beauty—and she was pretty handy with a 12-gauge too! Basically, my dream woman was standing right before me, and for the first time in a long time, it made me think about how important finding that perfect soul mate is to me.

I didn't hesitate to share my emotions. I wanted this to be my fairy tale come true.

On the final night we were together, sitting looking out over the serene Alabama pasture I've worked so hard to care for, I told her I loved her. She looked so beautiful in a white cotton dress, sitting in the tall grass. The sky turned dark purple as the sun dipped beneath the tree line.

My two geldings (arguably tired of overhearing all the sappy talk coming out of this cowboy's mouth) broke free of their reins and took off running over the sweeping hillsides. I just let them run, side by side, in full stride together. If ever there were a moment where I could see, and feel, true happiness, it was that moment: two horses, running full stride and free, in unison, into the sunset. Count. Me. In.

It seemed certain to end in the perfect fairy tale moment for me. I had used a word with a woman I had never used before.

Forever.

But I didn't get the girl.

I didn't find love. It wasn't my time. I've been bucked off many times before, but this kind of pain was so different from the pain

I was used to. I do believe, as Garth Brooks put it so perfectly, "Sometimes God's greatest gifts are unanswered prayers."

Looking back on it, I made so many lifelong, dear friends—both with my housemates and with the crew of the TV show. Those people with the ear pieces, I learned, had names and families. They'd come from all over the world, and by now we all knew each other like brothers.

And after she said "no," I never could have expected what came next: thousands and thousands of letters of support from all across this country.

When someone who doesn't know you takes the time to put down so many kind words and send them your way, I truly believe that's one of the greatest honors a cowboy can hope to achieve. Many of the letters were from women, cheering me on, and they had a similar theme: *We wish there were more real cowboys out there!*

And here is my answer to that—there are! There are lots of good guys out there; sometimes it's just a matter of getting them to "cowboy up" as we like to say.

That's why I decided to sit down and write out some of my thoughts. This book is about the cowboy philosophies I've been taught and how everyone can use them to find more happiness in your relationships and your daily life. It's about the little things that women can do to make sure they have a man who will act honorably, one who will treat them the way they deserve to be treated. It's about planning the right kind of dates to really get to know someone—and knowing it matters both at the start of a new romance, and in keeping a long-term relationship fresh and alive.

This book is about some of the common problems we all have and some of this cowboy's solutions to finding that partner to go through life with, in unison, at full stride.

2

ASK ABOUT THE FIRST LOVE

I'd never given much thought to what the cattle felt like, being shuffled and herded from one place to the next with people yapping and squawking at them from all sides, but that's exactly how it felt waking up in the *Sweet Home Alabama* house that first morning.

Twenty-two of us men were waking up and this was our first big day: We were going to meet the woman they had us all lined up to fight over.

There were "production" people everywhere, trying to get us all awake, dressed, and TV-ready. To be honest, I remain on the fence about what's the more difficult chore—moving a few hundred moaning cattle across the pasture as they wander off in different directions, or getting 22 guys dressed and ready to meet a girl.

One of the guys emptied an entire bottle of hairspray onto his head. The hissing sound lasted for ten minutes and sounded like a gas main had sprung a leak. You could feel the ozone layer under attack. It smelled like a cross between a high school locker room and the beauty parlor on Main Street. I've seen a lot of guys do a lot of things, but I suppose there is a first for everything. The kid's hair wasn't sprayed—it was shellacked. He topped it off with some cologne from a place called Chanel and a navy blazer that looked like a month's pay for a cowboy like me.

So this is the competition.

I fixed myself up all right and put on my hat. It was time.

All of us guys had been herded (literally) to a beautiful place called the Oak Hollow Farm. Farms are usually gritty places, but this one was all dressed up for special occasions and it did not disappoint. Beautiful meadows and bending oak trees surrounded the property. The pounding of running, wild horses would start and stop off in the distance. Fresh flowers; red, white, and blue bunting; sweet tea in Mason jars; and comfortable, handcrafted rocking chairs lined the shady, wrap-around porch. (A well-worn rocking chair is one of the great treasures of the South to me. Nothing can make you feel more at home.)

All I can say is there's a certain magic to Oak Hollow Farm. It's run by a salt-of-the-earth guy named Boyd and his family, who built the place. If you watch the show, you already know Boyd—he comes in now and then and browbeats the guys.

We were told as we waited that in a few moments the young woman would be driving up on the winding dirt road. When the breeze came through and I heard the fall leaves begin to rustle, I thought, "This is as good as any place for a fairy tale to begin."

Everyone—including me—had their eyes locked on the horizon.

We heard her before we saw her: A baby blue 1956 Ford pickup gurgled, the manual shifting gears ground slightly, going from first to second. It was the first sign that the time had come.

I could see the truck moving slowly in our direction, 22 men at the starting line of some kind of romantic sprint.

But I couldn't see her face.

The windshield was full of glare. The harder I squinted to see in, the more it looked like a reflection of the green and yellow leaves all around. The truck slowly wound toward us, kicking up dirt under the tires, the motor churning. The sight of leaves in the window slid up as the windshield moved toward us and sunlight ricocheted off the pale blue hood.

This is ridiculous, was all I could think.

More dust. More leaves. More glare. The pickup was closer now. It was going full speed, but it was all slow motion in that moment.

Am I going to regret this for the rest of my life?

Exactly how many counties—or states—away am I going to have to move before I hear the end of this?

Then I heard another voice inside my head, and it said something familiar:

Easy does it, cowboy. One step at a time.

Okay, I thought. That I knew how to do. That phrase has gotten me out of a bunch of jams in the past.

The classic old truck was close now. You could see the shiny chrome and the rust on the cowling around the headlights—but still no glimpse of the young lady behind the wheel. Was she blonde? Brunette? I couldn't tell. It was just more leaves going by and the reflection of the farm in the window.

The car was going about two miles an hour, but my mind was racing like Richard Petty around turn 4 at Daytona.

And, in that moment, I thought of Caroline, the first woman I ever loved.

And it was the type of falling in love that changed my life forever, in every possible way. Even though I was a very young man at the time, she taught me how to be in love. She taught me the best things about it.

In many ways, I was standing here on this dusty path of uncertainty, looking for the type of love I had with Caroline all those years ago.

In a moment I want to share the story of how we met, and how she changed my life. But before I do, I think that, looking back on everything, this might be the number one lesson—whether you're a woman trying to evaluate a guy you just met, or whether you're a guy out there in the dating world.

It's such a simple question, but we really do forget to ask it: *Are you looking for love?*

The lazy answer is "everyone is" or "we all want/need love." Maybe so. At least, that's what we're all told and led to believe.

But here's the more important question: "Is the guy or girl you're dating looking for love *RIGHT NOW right this moment?*" Because right now is when you need it. And if the answer to that question is "no," if his/her heart isn't seeking what yours is seeking, then my advice is to not send another text and not waste another breath— you need and deserve someone who's looking for love.

When a truck with a mysterious silhouette of a girl I'd never met before was driving at me, and I *instinctively* thought back to the first time I was ever in love and ever said those words looking into someone's eyes, that was a sign I was sending to myself—a voice saying *you want this* and *you need this in your life again.*

Hurry up and get to it!

Again, it wasn't a voice saying, *"You miss Caroline"* or *"You want Caroline,"* it was a need saying, *"You miss that!"*

For women especially, this is my number one rule for you all: You want to find a guy who wants and misses that in his world. Now the question becomes, how can you get at that information?

Well, this is advice no one ever gives, but here goes: When the moment is right, ask him about the first time he fell in love.

Let him tell you the story. *And do not get jealous of the girl in the story he is about to tell.*

You have no reason to be jealous of her at all. He's not in love with her. She taught him about the most idealistic kinds of love. You're about to unlock that in him and be the beneficiary of all of that good stuff.

He's probably going to tell you a story that happened to him when he was late in his teens or early in his twenties. The girl in the story might have passionately loved him back or might not have given him the time of day. It doesn't matter. For him, this is how he first learned what love is and fixed in his mind how he wanted it to be.

As the song says, *"that's something that just don't happen twice."*

It might take a little patience to get the story out of him, and like I said, the timing is going to have to be just right. Please don't try this with SportsCenter on, or while he is loading his golf clubs in the trunk about to head out with his buddies, or when he's trying to unlock the next map on *Call of Duty*.

You can and should ask it early on though. Find the time and make him tell you the story. You're sending him an important signal in the process: "I'm not the jealous type" and "I understand there are other people in your world." You're saying, "I'm confident in myself that I can accept you've loved before because with me, it's going to be the best love of your life."

Even though the story ends badly, or in a bittersweet place for him, if you listen, he's giving you the roadmap to how his heart worked when it was at its very best. That girl in the story? Don't hate her or be jealous of her—she did you an enormous favor. This woman is your friend. When you say her name or ask about her, use her name and speak it fondly. It's going to make you appear more confident to him and let him know his past is something you accept, that every other woman isn't "her" or "that old girlfriend of yours."

And, if he's' still in truly in love with her, you're about to know it—and better to know it now.

If he can't answer the question, refuses to talk about his feelings, shrugs you off or ignores you, there's a good chance he is NOT looking for love, and you may as well know that right here and now before another beautiful sunset drops over the tree line.

But, if you see a little glimmer in his eye, a smile, or a look as he tells the story; if he gets a little wistful, emotional, and even shy, then he will have answered that most important question of all: Is he looking for love?

He might even say, "I'm still waiting to be in love for the first time." That's your answer, too.

There's no wrong answer to this question. The only wrong answer is no answer at all.

There is no downside to asking a man to tell you about the first time he fell in love.

So, here comes an old truck with a strange girl I can't even get a decent look at, and it's already reminding me of the first time I fell, and fell hard.

How many dates do I go on before I "move on"?

Sometimes I hear people say they are looking for that feeling of butterflies and adrenaline. That's what they are craving. That's how they describe wanting to be in love.

I think the spirit of that exhilaration comes from a place of sweetness. I truly do.

But there might be another way to look at it. Some of those things – butterflies and a rush – you can get on thrill ride at a theme park. And those thrill rides tend to have sharp twists and turns, and sudden drops from the sky. Sometimes they make you queasy in the end.

Lately I have been convinced that – above all – true love should bring you peace.

Sometimes being near someone brings you a sense of peace and calm. Just being near them makes you feel safe.

No matter where you happen to be at that moment, when that person is around, you feel at home.

There are times when I hear people question whether they are "into" someone or if "the spark is there" or whether the "butterflies" are there or not.

I think that might be the wrong question to be asking yourself so early on. If you have a sense of true peace when you are with that other person, keep going out with them. If you feel like you can be yourself around that person, keep going out with them.

If it can be quiet for long stretches of time, but it is a peaceful sense of calm and quiet – keep going out with them.

Angels are sent to us to bring us peace and hope and care for us, not give us butterflies, and take sudden turns.

3

BEING GENEROUS

She was my high school sweetheart, and her name was Caroline.

It was the start of my 11th grade year, and we were sitting in the auditorium at West Orange High School—me, Billy Joe, and my buddy, Scott—and all the new kids and everybody else were coming in, getting their schedules.

We didn't have the right schedules for our classes and stuff, so we were sitting there waiting on them to give us our class schedule. And all of a sudden, this cute little brown-headed, blue-eyed, confident young lady comes walking in, and me and Scott and Billy are like, "Oh, my word."

She walked by and she had the prettiest smile. I was like, "Oh, my gosh. Who is that?"

They didn't know—we had no idea. I told them boys, "I'm gonna date her, you watch."

Well, a couple days go by and she winds up dating this boy we knew named Dustin. We all could sense there was something a little off about him, but they dated for quite a few months. When

I would go from third period to my history class every day, I'd pass them, and every time I passed them, she would look at me and you could tell he would get a little jealous because she was looking over my way.

I remember one day, I walked past them and they were fighting about something. He was hollering and pointing in her face. So, I just stopped and said, "Hey, you don't deserve that. You just leave him and come on, be with me, and you won't be treated like that," and I went on about my business.

That was on a Monday or Tuesday, and I think she wound up splitting up with him that weekend. We got together the next week, going to dinner and stuff like that. And I just completely fell in love, head-over-heels for her. We dated for about five years—a long time.

Every afternoon my dad didn't have me working was an afternoon we'd spend together. Every weekend we'd be together. We were Bubba-and-Caroline at school and around town. The preps had their couple, the nerds had their couple, and then you had the country folks that had their couple, and she and I were the country side of the deal.

She was probably like five foot four, five foot five, athletic build, beautiful legs, beautiful body; she was just gorgeous. She was a little country girl—loved to hunt, loved to fish, ride four-wheelers, get dirty. She was tough too, you know, they've got to be a little tough! She was tough and had grit to her.

We'd do anything together—just ride dirt roads, go mudding— and we had a special place we'd go, especially on Friday and Saturday nights.

It was a perfect, magical little spot on a lake, and that's where some of my fondest times with Caroline happened. Lake Sawyer is the name of it, and it was down Florida State Road 535—a dusty road that led out of town. The road splits at one point and takes you to the main entrance to Walt Disney World, but if you stay on 535 the other way, it takes you around back, to the charming little lake just around back. No one except the locals knows it's there. There's just orange grove after orange grove, pastures, and fields. That's where I grew up as a kid.

We would get on the 535 and go out to the lake and get out there on the dock where we could fish. It was a beautiful lake, with cypress trees all the way around it. It was a breath of fresh air, especially with her there. It was just amazing—that clear, clean air and orange blossoms blooming in the springtime. I don't know if you've ever smelled an orange blossom, but it's amazing.

Thinking about it just makes me happy.

We'd fish there all the time. There were also some hogs out there, so we'd go out there and try to catch hogs with our dogs and things like that. Or we'd just sit right next to each other with our feet hanging off the deck like she and I were the only things in the world that existed.

You know, there was nothing else to worry about except she and I being together. That's all there was to it. I wanted to be with her all the time, and she wanted to be with me all the time.

It was just peaceful.

There was also a swing out there on the dock, and sometimes we'd just sit there and hear the waves and the water crashing up against the shoreline. We'd talk for hours and I decided, even as a young man, to be as generous as I could be with my feelings and emotions and affections. (And there was a lot of that going on on that remote, wooden pier on Lake Sawyer.)

I guess I have a big heart, and when I'm with someone, I care about how she feels. I think women should be treated with respect. I think they should be loved on, 'cause I was loved on as a kid. My mom and dad always took care of me.

My dad always hugged me, even if there were tons of men around or whatever—I was just always in an affectionate family, and I think that's why I am the way that I am. To this day, when I see my nieces, nephews, and sisters, I always hug 'em and kiss 'em. I mean that's just a sign of love, you know? Public displays of affection should be encouraged because that just shows you're a loving and caring person and people respect that.

So anyway, back to Lake Sawyer and Caroline and me. The sun would go down in a bright orange sunset, and we'd fish for a little while longer. We had a light that would hang over the dock to bring the bait fish in so we could catch the big fish.

When nine o'clock rolled around, that first boom would go off, and it made my heart skip every time. The dock we were on was just on the other side of the fence from Disney World, and on the weekends they would light up the sky with the biggest fireworks show you've ever seen. Loud, bright, colorful, and we had the perfect, private, front-row seat. Every weekend was like that for Caroline and me.

Right over our heads you could see 'em—boom!—the big fireworks.

Crack! Like stars shooting in the sky. They reflected in the water, all those colors glimmering on the pond.

The best view, though, was the light on her face—red, silver, yellow—she looked perfect in all of them as the night lit up, then went dark again, over and over. You want to know the best way to enjoy fireworks? Watch them sparkle in a beautiful woman's eyes right next to you.

We'd sit there and watch the fireworks on the dock and do a little kissing, or just go to the truck and talk some more.

But I didn't tell her that I loved her until we went to prom, and by then, we'd been dating for a long time—I don't ever just throw that word out. We probably dated eight or nine months before I'd ever said that.

We went to prom and we were just slow dancing, and I think the dance was coming to an end. I just looked at her and told her that I loved her, and she said, "I love you, too."

From then on it was something that we always said to each other, you know? We meant it and a part of me will always love her because she was my first love. She's great and I did everything in the world for her, and she did the same for me. She always made me feel loved and I always made her feel loved.

Then the day came toward the end of school when she called me and told me that she needed to talk to me. She had mentioned to me several times that she may be going off to school, and I just thought she would go to school around here. Her daddy, though, was big on the idea of her going to college, and he wanted her to go off to a good school.

She called me, told me that she needed to talk to me, and came out to the house. We were upstairs in my bedroom, at my dad's old house, when she told me that she was going to go away to school. She'd picked Auburn, where her mom had gone to school.

Are you wondering how I took it? I just hit the floor crying, to be honest with you. I didn't want to see her go. That was tough.

She started crying and told me that since she'd gotten accepted to Auburn and would be going off to school, there wouldn't be any way that she and I could continue our relationship up there. I understood that, you know? Hell, that's a long ways away.

I thought my whole world was coming to an end because the love of my life had to go off and go to school. But I knew she had to do it. I just couldn't bear the thought of her dating someone else. That just drove me nuts.

Even though we stayed in contact, I was devastated. My dad was worried about me for a while because he said there were days that went by when I didn't come out of my room. I was upset, and unless I had to come out to get something to eat or something, I would just sit up there in my room all the time. It was almost like somebody died in the family. I wouldn't get to see her anytime soon. It was my first love and my first heartbreak. The two so often go hand in hand, and that's the truth.

What's the miracle cure for the heartbreak?

Time, to be honest with you. Time's about the only thing. A lot of people will tell you to get out—that the easiest way to get over someone is to get up and get underneath another one, but I don't agree with that one bit. They say, "Well, if this one broke your heart, just go find another one real quick," but that doesn't cure your heartache. It doesn't work like that.

For a time, I was sitting around the house, thinking there was a chance she may just pull into my driveway this weekend and come stay with me, or that I'd get a call from her saying that she had decided not to go to school anymore. I held out hope for a long time, but the more I heard from her and knew about what she was doing, the more I was forced to find some closure.

Over time, she was honest with me about what was going on and what she was doing, and I was honest with her about what I was doing too. She started dating another guy a couple months into college, and we talked things over. It was the only way to handle it, and it did help me. I mean, it hurt me in a way too, but it helped me through and gave me some of the closure I needed.

Only later did I realize how lucky was I to have met her, loved her, and to have had her treat me so well when the time came to heal and move on. As for the feelings, I can sit here and tell you that I put it in a box and locked it up and it went away, but that's not true. It doesn't go away. Caroline was my first real, true love.

And I think about that sky full of fireworks all the time.

Home

Another good question to ask a guy is, *what makes him feel at home?*

We all have a place – a creek or a meadow, a trail or a living room sofa, a hillside or a winding dirt road – the taste of a particular cola or beer, the sound of a familiar stream or wind through the branches of a favorite tree outside a window -- that makes us feel at home.

However he answers this question will tell you about how to put him at ease, and once you have him in that place – that's where you are most likely to succeed in getting a guy to open up, and speak to you from the heart.

I hate to compare us to cattle but in this case it kind of fits.

When you are weaning a baby calf away from its momma that's a really touchy process. Here you have a kid that's about a year old, and it follows that mom around for its entire childhood, and now for the first time you are going to separate him and put him out there on his own.

That little cow will cry all night sometimes trying to get back to the only home it knows – right there at its mother's side. It wants to feel at home.

You can take a baby cow miles away from its momma, and it'll somehow find its way through the woods back to the last spot it was at when they were together.

Those first couple days are very stressful on the little calves and we have to do everything we can to keep them calm and healthy.

To some extent, I think the same thing happens to a guy, as he is growing up. We identify with places and sounds, and tastes and sights, and these make us feel safe and at home. When we are there we aren't as jumpy and alert as we have to be out and about. It gets in our DNA.

You can work a horse all day long on the hottest day of the year. He will go for hours through the thickets and the briars. He can be sweating right through the darn saddle. But when he gets sight of that barn I promise you he will find a whole other gear and fly over that pasture one stride stronger than the next. He wants to be home.

This is why, if you have something important to say to us, sometimes a restaurant or in the car on the way home from the movie theater isn't the best place to do it.

Go there and you will see how much easier it is to make that deeper connection.

Soon, when you ask him where he feels most at home, he will say *"next to you"*.

4

LOOK THEM IN THE EYE AND SPEAK FROM THE HEART

The pale blue pickup rolled to a stop and you could tell by the way she stepped out of the car the young woman was humble and kind. The way she moved and slightly quivered let us all know she was just as nervous as we were.

She had long dark hair, and for a moment I could see that girl in 11th grade walking past me in the auditorium. But no, this girl was much different, and this situation sure as heck was much different.

A bunch of guys competing for one girl.

We all had turned over our phones and computers and had no TVs, and we'd all set aside three or four weeks of time. We all had so much in common. Without all of the modern-day distractions, it was a certainty that out of this large group of guys, all focused on one girl, true feelings would develop. But who would it be, and would those feelings be returned?

This was no way for a grown man to fall in love, but when I saw her face, her eyes, and the way she humbly walked up the steps, it all just hit me that the time was right. I was already falling for *the idea* of being in love. Now the question was, *is she the girl?*

Her name was Paige.

We had already been told, behind the scenes, that there was a chance that the young lady we were going to meet had something in her past that fell under the heading of a "lapse in judgment" or "moment of personal weakness."

We were all asked ahead of time, "If a girl in your life has made a serious mistake or embarrassed herself in some way by a decision in her past, is this something you can forgive?"

In order to make it this far, we all had to answer "yes," we have forgiveness in our hearts. What is in the past is in the past. You make mistakes and you learn from them. This is part of the Cowboy Code—having forgiveness in your heart. (We'll talk more about the specifics of the Cowboy Code a bit later.)

In Paige's case, as we were about to learn, she had famously texted provocative photos of herself to a former boyfriend in a moment of weakness as an attempt to keep his attention. Later in life, when she was chosen by NASCAR to be one of their top spokesmodels, the photos got posted on the Internet. It was a devastating embarrassment for her and her family, in the small Southern town of Lancaster, South Carolina. The photos were everywhere.

To this day I haven't seen them myself, but they are described as particularly upsetting. Some of the guys in the group knew about her and knew about the photos.

The result was, despite her apologies, NASCAR and their sponsors let her go. It was a dream job, traveling the country trackside with the top drivers in the world—a front-row seat to the greatest spectacles in racing: Daytona, Charlotte Motor Speedway, Bristol, Talladega. Her mistake cost her dearly. It was all gone in a split second.

It had been about six months since the scandal. At the moment we were all inclined to give her the benefit of the doubt. There was something appealing about her being a woman in distress, needing someone strong to stand by her side. All the guys agreed that we would never bring up the indiscretion of the photos on the Internet.

It was a perfect day for a fresh start for everyone.

When she got around to the front of that truck, facing down 22 guys, she spoke about how God had put her through some trials in her life, but how when one door closes it can lead you to something more meaningful. She told us, her voice quivering, that she truly was here because it was part of a higher plan.

Something wonderful had been taken from her life. Could something even more meaningful have been meant for her instead? In my opinion, this was a wonderful way to take a horrible situation and find a higher meaning in it all. First impressions are important, and as far as I was concerned, this was a near-perfect first impression. A woman looking for that higher meaning, well, that's one of the most beautiful qualities you can have—and if you can talk about it with a sweet Southern drawl—well then, that's gonna get this cowboy's attention right out of the gate every time!

I can get used to that real quick! I thought to myself.

She giggles and smiles, sometimes from nerves, sometimes from uncontrollable happiness. She has that Southern way about her of making you feel right at home, even though you've just said "hello"—and with 21 other sharks circling around waiting to meet her too.

But today, the other guys didn't matter. When the time came, I took a few paces away from the group, sat her down on a picnic table, and said, "My name's Bubba!"

What came next was very unexpected for me, but it was a pretty decent lesson—I had to introduce myself in pretty much two minutes or less. I mean, the way I'm used to it, if you sit down with a pretty lady, you can take your time and really get to know her. You can talk and let the conversation meander. But this was a different animal here, and I wasn't prepared for it. It was the equivalent of the two-minute drill in football, where the clock is counting down at the end of the game, you have no time-outs, no huddles, and you have to lead the offense 80 yards to the score.

And I'd gone out on the field with nothing—I hadn't rehearsed anything in my mind to say.

If I had another piece of advice to give, it would involve this two-minute drill. Go look in the mirror and pretend you're describing yourself to someone new. Convey your essence to them in a handful of sentences. It's really hard, but it's also really easy.

It's difficult in that we all tend to judge or censor or doubt ourselves, or we couch some of our opinions. At some level we're all thinking, "What does the other person want to hear? What will they want me to say?"

But that's not the cowboy way.

A cowboy will look you in the eye and speak from the heart.

I use this in business all the time. Instead of small talk and chatter, just say what you want and what you expect, and more often than not you'll get your way. Or, you'll know immediately that this deal isn't the right one for you. (In my opinion, America could use a lot more straight talking, right about now.)

So, on that picnic table, after she sweetened up my name and said "Buuuubaaa!!!" (It sounded so much better in her accent than mine!) I kind of looked up from underneath my black Stetson hat and said the obvious.

"I'm a cowboy from Geneva, Alabama."

"Oh, I've had bad luck with cowboys," she said.

Ouch!

"I've had cowboys break my heart," she added.

"I'm not that kind of cowboy. I'm a ranch cowboy," I explained.

This is a big distinction, and I probably should've explained it to you all a little earlier as well. There are lots of different kinds of cowboys. People hear "cowboy" and think of the brave and daring guys who rodeo for a living, like the bull-riders and the calf-ropers. Some of my best friends are rodeo cowboys and they're awesome people.

Some of these guys on the circuit, they go from town to town, from paycheck to paycheck. A rodeo cowboy lives his life on the road, you know? Fast women and pretty horses, as they like to say, lights and rodeos and loud noise.

He's in one city this week. He may be in another state the next weekend. The rodeo lifestyle's glamorous, but it's not a secure lifestyle. One day you may have $2,000 in your pocket. The next day, you may owe somebody $2,000.

The rodeo cowboy spends all of his money just to get to that rodeo, and if he doesn't win, he doesn't eat. He may not even be able to get home from that rodeo if he doesn't win, you know? They put all their money on the line just to make a little bit more money.

But I'm what they call a ranch cowboy. I buy, sell, trade, and raise cattle for a living on my ranch in Geneva, Alabama. I buy, trade, raise, and sell horses there as well.

A ranch cowboy gets up every morning and gets out with his horse and he goes to work. He works until the job's done, and then he goes home and lies in bed at night and gets up the next morning and does the same thing. The ranch cowboy's a day-in day-out job. It's security, or at least as much as you can get when you're raising cattle and horses.

From daylight to dark (or we like to call it from "can to can't"), you work from the time you can see the sun come up on the horizon to the time after it sets on the other side of the pasture.

I don't run up and down the road all the time. I'm at my place. I wake up every morning, go to work, and I come home every night. I work six, seven days a week.

Paige has had a lot of misconceptions and had her heart broken by guys that rodeo because those guys are in a different town every night and—different town, different women, different area codes. That's how some people act. And that's how some people think. But it isn't the way I live.

I'm on horseback all the time—pretty much from daylight to dark. And if I'm not horseback, I'm in the pasture, messing with the cattle, or I'm at the barn with the horses. I'm constantly doing something, and I always look over at my house and the empty garage and think, I just wish there was a beautiful woman here that I could come home to and cook dinner for and just love—a woman to start a family with.

There have been many, many an hour and many, many nights and nights of going to bed by myself, just dreaming of that kind of life. As a group, cowboys don't want to talk about their feelings. But a lot of us feel this way. Cowboys always put God first, and then family. After that, you just live your life one day at a time, ready to tackle anything that comes your way. We're not scared of anything, and it's a rough life—it's not for the weak.

Without a woman in my life right now, and after God and family, the dearest things that I hold next to my heart are my horses; they're my best friends. I spend my whole life with them.

I'm proud to be a cowboy; I wouldn't want to do anything else. I may not die a rich man, but I'm going to die a happy man. I'm going to die a happy man doing what I love to do—cowboying for the rest of my life—ranching, buying, and trading cattle; roping off horses; training horses; anything that has to do with that is what I'm all about.

Cowboys are the last of a dying breed. It's a long tradition, and there aren't many of us left in this world. I'm excited and very proud to be one. I've learned from a lot of good other cowboys, and I take everything that they taught me and try to put it into my everyday life. Good cowboys are hard to find. We're providers. It's something that's hard to describe, and a lot of people don't understand it. But I've got a lot of pride, and I'm very honored to be an American cowboy.

***

So there you have it. That's pretty much my life in two minutes or less! This is another tip I would give you—guy or girl, even though I'm not a believer in speed dating or anything like that—prepare to describe yourself really quickly and what's at your core. The Southern way is to take your time, really get to know the essence of the other person. Reserve judgment, and have an open mind.

When it comes to relationships, my experience is your instincts are the most valuable tools you have. But you may as well be the most effective communicator you can be right from the outset. So whether your first date is a long walk, or dinner and a movie, or a cup of overpriced coffee in one of those expensive places, my advice is, before you say goodbye, prepare to present yourself in two minutes or so to the other person. Come to the table and lay down your cards.

It's worth asking yourself the questions, "Who am I? Who do I want to be?" This isn't about the kind of car you drive or the fancy restaurants you've eaten at. If your mind went there first, maybe spend some time soul searching. Before you're ready to get into a real relationship, you need to have an answer to those questions. The faster you communicate this to someone you're interested in, the better off you both are going to feel.

Here's how my two minutes went with Paige:

BUBBA:	I have a ranch over in South Alabama.
PAIGE:	Okay.
BUBBA:	I love it. I'm on horseback all day, every day.
PAIGE:	Yeah? I love—
BUBBA:	Do you ride?
PAIGE:	Yes, I do. I—
BUBBA:	I do too. I ... I'm goin' kind of nuts, you know? 'cause I hadn't rode in a while—
PAIGE:	Yeah.
BUBBA:	But it's well worth the wait.
PAIGE:	(To Camera) Bubba is just the cowboy that you read about in romantic novels. He is a man's man, a rugged cowboy. He just melts my heart. And I love horses. There's like something about—the outside of a horse that's good for the inside of a person—
BUBBA:	Love.
PAIGE:	Yeah.
BUBBA:	Yeah. I love 'em. And I'm—
PAIGE:	Me too.

BUBBA:	On 'em all the time and—
PAIGE:	Mm-hmm.
BUBBA:	I've got six of 'em myself, and I run about 3,000 head of cattle.
PAIGE:	Yeah.
BUBBA:	I'm a busy guy.
PAIGE:	Yeah, a busy guy.
BUBBA:	All the time. Yeah. You know? I wouldn't trade it for anything.
PAIGE:	(To Camera) Mm-hmm. I love his accent. He has pretty blue eyes. His cowboy hat. He was one of the easiest to talk to.
BUBBA:	I'm a big family-oriented person.
PAIGE:	Mm-hmm.
BUBBA:	I think that's the most important thing in life. Without a family, you really don't have anything, you know? So that's the main thing in my life—
PAIGE:	Mm-hmm.
BUBBA:	You know, family and God.
BUBBA:	(To Camera) Paige is definitely the girl to get you off the horse and get you home and spend time with.
PAIGE:	I'm glad you're here.
BUBBA:	Nice talking to you.

After my two minutes were up, Paige looked at me at the end of the conversation and said, "Okay, I'm gonna give you a chance."

All I could was look at her big brown eyes.

5

Don't Get Caught in the Drama

We were several days into the taping period, and the first of the private dates had already happened. Guys were getting picked to venture off and have private time with Paige, and they were coming back to the house, talking about how they were enraptured.

Some had confided they'd kissed her and it was the most romantic moment of their lives.

For real?

Some of these private trips took place on farms, out on the lakes, and in the cotton fields. One of the other guys was a farmer, and he had asked to take her on a combine. There had also been a series of group-type outings, and on those everyone got some quiet time to get to know Paige.

So by know I knew her through a series of my own little asides, and—oddly—by listening to other guys talk after they'd come home from romantic evenings out and about.

It was the strangest possible way to get to know someone. Everyone came home glowing from spending time with Paige. There was so much free time that talking about her became an obsession. I found myself getting to know a woman through the eyes of other men, and there's nothing normal about that.

The down time we had and the scant details that came back from the field had a dual role: First, it inspired your competitive juices and made you want to engage just to win. Secondly it gave your mind time to wander off to its own vision of a romantic place. And the more time you spent there in your mind, the more you wanted to get there in real life.

Before long, the first couple of waves of guys had been sent home, eliminated, crushed, and devastated.

Old Boyd from the Oak Hollow Farm would come in every few days, pace across the wrap-around porch, dress us all down, and then tap the vulnerable among us on the shoulder to walk out and learn if you were getting a second chance, or getting the gate.

When you see it on TV, you wonder how people can get so attached and emotional. Trust me—it's every bit as intense in person as it is on your TV screen.

Everyone gets so hopeful, and it hurts to be rejected; that's why you see the tears in my opinion. It isn't love or heartbreak: It's the rapid-fire shifting of gears from hope and optimism to rejection. It's the whiplash effect of hearing "no" and having to pack up your things and move out. Everything's so compressed—time, space, living quarters, and emotions.

As I watched it all around me, I was convinced that would never happen to me. It wasn't arrogance speaking; I just kept focusing on the positive. I would look out at that view over Mobile Bay and relax. *Let the others get caught up in the melodrama*, I'd think. *That stuff ain't for me.*

A lot of us were becoming friends, but as you might expect, there were a couple of exceptions to the rule. One of them took place in the form of a person unlike any I'd met before: Shaun Bigos. And he was looking to get jacked in the face from the moment he stepped off the plane.

The whole competition amongst us guys centered on us country guys versus a bunch of city guys, and Shaun was the biggest and loudest of the city types, from the biggest and loudest city of all, the concrete jungle of New York City.

SHAUN B: (To Camera) These hillbillies are funny. They all look alike. I think they're brothers.

SHAUN B: (To Camera) I could care less what they think. I mean, I live in New York City. I have a very thick skin.

A cowboy can't provide for a female, okay? You gotta have a home.

No girl is gonna wanna eat beans every single day. I mean, I wouldn't.

I do believe that people in the country are drunk. They're just trashy people in my mind. Down here, it's too slow. I mean, I don't wanna sit out by a campfire and drink real cheap beer every single night. That's just not me.

He came reeking of cologne and arrogance, calling us all hillbillies. In his words, cowboys were a bunch of penniless nothings who sit around a campfire eating baked beans, and people from the South were slow-minded alcoholics who dated within their own families. This is literally what he believed.

SHAUN B: (To Camera) Because I don't smell like horse manure, I guess, they got really upset. So I guess if I smelled like [bleep] they'd be real happy about it. But because I wear Chanel, I guess, I smell like a pretty boy. I don't know.

We had all signed a contract promising that whatever differences we had, we wouldn't take them out physically on one another. But try talking like that almost anywhere else in the South and you're liable to have your jaw jacked and ass whipped. Down here, we aren't shy, and when you run your mouth a little, your whole world can change, as they say, in a New York minute.

Shaun is the definition of a pampered city slicker.

One day—before going camping, no less—I walked by and he was right in front of this big old mirror. He must have been sitting there for 45 minutes, getting his hair ready, and he must have used a whole can of hairspray. As I walked by, I said, "Shaun, how much hairspray you go through a week?"

He said, "Uh, about eight bottles."

I said, "Eight bottles of hairspray? Dude, I got four sisters and I bet a can will last them a month."

He said, "Well, yeah, I ain't your sister."

He even asked one of the producers if they could take a special trip into town so he could get his eyebrows waxed—after going to the tanning salon. I was thinking, if Paige was on a date with him and reached down to hold his hand, she might have to do a double-take, wondering if it's a chick she's holding onto.

In all reality, I think he'd make one hell of a housewife.

First off, this cowboy ain't going to get his eyebrows waxed. I sure ain't going to get my toes done or my nails done. I'm rough and rugged, you know? I am what I am.

This cowboy here ain't sitting down in no salon. Where I come from, the men just don't do that. I like to be scruffy. That's just me and that's my personality. Cowboys are supposed to be tough, and I'm one tough son of a gun. It was going to take mental toughness—and patience—to get rid of Shaun Bigos and the others like him, and I knew just how to do it.

Every now and again in a herd of cattle, one will go crazy on you. You go out in the pasture and it'll just run wildly. When you get one of these in the herd, you have to get rid of it. It's likely to hurt you or one of your men, and it'll keep the other cattle all riled up and stressed.

The best way to track these 1,200-pound spastic cattle is to get out there in the thick bush—and just wait on it. Whatever it takes, you just sit there real quiet, on your horse, backed up into the deep scrub. The thicker the brush is beneath you and the tree limbs around you, the better.

Sooner or later that dumb-ass steer or bull will walk through there like they own the place. And then you get the joy of springing on them when they least expect it. Your horse will tear out of those weeds, and you turn on that animal and scare the daylights out of it. You get it when it least expects you to be there.

It may be 1,400 pounds and you may be 165, but you have the advantage. In that moment you have to be ready to swing your rope, fire that loop around its neck, and choke it to the ground. I've done that move about a hundred times, and it feels wonderful.

I was going to wait for my chance to do it to big Cro-Magnon man Shaun Bigos, for sure.

SHAUN B: (To Camera) A real man is somebody who is cultured, professional, intelligent, good head on their shoulders, provides for the family, doesn't shovel [bleep] all day.

The other guys squabbled and squawked at him, and he loved rolling around in the verbal mud with them. Mouth off to a New Yorker, and they've got you on their turf. These people run their mouths just to get from Starbucks to the damn subway. I could never live like that.

I just decided to take a little cover, back up into some thick woods, and wait for my moment to loop his neck.

***

The next morning we woke up and there was a vintage, 1958 black Ford pickup truck parked in the driveway. It was a classic from end to end, with wood trim and original leather bench seats up front.

All of us guys walked out to see her. On the windshield, underneath the wiper, was a little old pink card. It had my name on it.

The note read:

> *Dear Bubba, I would love for you to take me out this afternoon. Can you plan something and come pick me up?*
>
> *Love, Paige*

I had planned an evening to remember, just for the occasion.

It was a calm fall evening, which in the South means you get the best of all worlds: a warm afternoon to enjoy the sunshine without the oppressive heat and humidity of summer, followed by a crisp night to bundle up in after the sun went down. There was hardly a cloud in the sky; it was just perfect.

I picked her up around five o'clock and, trailed by two vans full of cameramen and producers (which made me laugh 'cause in my world a producer is a cow that breeds a new calf every year without missing one—which we call "going open" for the mating season). Anyway, off we went to Paige's house to go calling on her.

And yes, I'll admit now, for the first time I was a little nervous. The little butterflies were just starting to flutter.

She hopped in that old truck, the engine growled to life, and she asked me, "Where are we goin' Bubba?" only when she says it, it sounds much more beautiful than it reads on the page. The girl's accent made even the simplest sentences sound like a song: The word "goin'" was stretched out to about twelve syllables on the high end of the musical scale, and then there was the way she said "Bubba," which fluttered up and down a bunch of times like a two-lane state road cutting across hilly terrain.

I wasn't telling her. I wanted it to be a surprise. Some things I'm pretty sure about and some things I'm just guessing, but I'm pretty sure every girl likes surprises. Even little ones get them going.

I pulled up to a stretch of beach at the west end of the town of Fairhope, Alabama, where we were staying. There's a one-mile stretch of white sand where the bay gently laps up at the shore. And on most days, like that day, there was no one else around.

At the end of the drive, I had two quarter horses saddled and waiting with the reins lashed around a tree. Our friend Boyd from the Oak Hollow Farm had hooked me up with the horses, a favor from one cowboy to another. (Cowboys always help each other.)

We got up on horseback and instantly I knew the girl could ride. She wasn't going to be okay with just walking or trotting along;

she dug in her heels and that horse took off. I'd be lying if I said it didn't get my complete attention.

It occurred to me that in all my years of riding, and I mean countless days of dusk-till-dawn on the back of a horse, I'd never ridden on the beach before. I spend a lot of my riding time dodging trees, or on rocks or the hard-packed open fields and pastures around Southeastern Alabama. Every bump finds its way up through that saddle, and there are times when you can feel every move in all the bones in your body.

But it was different riding on the beach. This felt a whole lot more like floating on air—or maybe it felt like that because of the beautiful girl next to me running stride for stride. This is how it went for us:

> PAIGE: I'm glad you were patient.
>
> BUBBA: Absolutely. Nice to get out of the house and be with you, you know?

When I saw her on that paint horse, I knew right there that she was a true cowgirl.

> BUBBA: I like this, don't you?
>
> PAIGE: Me too, on the beach—I've never ridden on the beach. Have you?
>
> BUBBA: Never.
>
> PAIGE: Never? Me either.
>
> BUBBA: No, this is a first.
>
> PAIGE: (To Camera) Every book I read, every movie I see, all my favorites involve a cowboy, and this girl falls in love with him and riding horses every day.

BUBBA:	Got plenty of reins in your hand?
PAIGE:	I got it.
BUBBA:	All right, well, take off.
PAIGE:	Okay, let's try this.
PAIGE:	Oh God! [LAUGHS] Oh God! Little bit of buckin'! [LAUGHS] It's okay. He can't kick, he can't buck.
PAIGE:	(To Camera) We're just like trottin' up and down the beach and then we start runnin' and my horse is buckin' and I'm just laughin'. [LAUGHS]
BUBBA:	(To Camera) Her horse bucked a little bit. She hung on. You know, it kinda turned me on. I was feeling a little fresh myself, you know? My neck's swellin' up, lip curlin' a little bit, you know? She, she's just a wonderful person.
PAIGE:	Race ya.
BUBBA:	(To Camera) That ride along the beach was the most romantic thing that I've ever done in my entire life.
PAIGE:	We're like synchronized riders now.
BUBBA:	(To Camera) Definitely feel some major emotions for her right now.

One thing about a cowboy—he doesn't beat around the bush or try to sugarcoat anything. He'll just tell you exactly what he's feeling, but we usually don't do all that well when it comes to the mushy stuff, emotions or feelings. I wasn't even expecting much of that on a first date, but seeing a beautiful woman like that on a horse riding along the water's edge—it got my blood flowing. As I later said to one of the TV crew following us, "It got me frisky."

The horses stopped and I pulled alongside her as the sun was going down over the bay, and we had our first kiss—soft and sweet. The horses held perfectly still, but inside, I felt like we were running at a full gait. The front creases of our cowboy hats wound around and brushed each other as our heads leaned in. She has wide, forgiving eyes, and you can't truly appreciate their deep brown color until you're really that close up.

It was such a romantic moment for me. My heart didn't just skip a beat—it skipped a bunch of them. In that moment I knew that, despite the absurdity of the situation, I was going to fight for this feeling as hard as I could.

And the date wasn't even over, not by a country mile.

With the sun down and the temperature dropping, we walked up the beach and came upon a bonfire I'd built. It was a big, tall fire right out there on the sand with a bunch of blankets and pillows pushed against a log out there in the open. That fire was glowing orange.

To me, this is the ultimate front-row seat. A warm fire and a bottle of wine—call me simple, but I don't need anything more than that.

We spent the better part of an hour cuddled up together, keeping warm. There were stories about her family and mine, and more kisses.

And in between there was some silence.

You know you're meant to be around someone when it gets quiet and it isn't awkward at all. You aren't "trying" or putting on a front when you can sit and be still, and in the moment, you aren't trying to be anything other than yourself. A good question to ask yourself in a relationship is, "Can we be around each other when it's still and quiet?" If you answer yes, that's a great sign you're with the right person.

I hate to compare people to cattle (especially at a romantic moment like this), but do you know how you can tell if a cow is healthy and strong? The happiest ones are the ones who are lying down and still in a nice comfortable spot. They have no stress in them; they're happy in the moment. Those are the ones who are going to make you money.

The same thing holds true in relationships for me. If you can be still next to someone and it feels good, that's a sign there's a lot of happiness that's going to come in the future. It means you're in balance.

The fire was crackling, embers flying. It was perfect to sit there and just talk, whisper, kiss, and be still. The sky had turned a deep purple and there was one more surprise to be had. I reached under the pillow and grabbed a two-way radio I'd hidden there, waiting for the perfect moment.

I keyed the mic and said, "Fire in the hole, cowboy!"

The sky lit up. Fireworks rocketed upwards from the pier, reaching out over the water.

"No way!" she screamed.

They cracked and boomed high over the bay as the water glimmered and reflected the lights above. It was like watching in stereo—one sky-bound explosion after the next! And I had a beautiful girl, beaming and giggling out of control, next to me in my arms.

This felt right to me for so many reasons. In some ways it was a callback to the past, to being a teenager and sitting on the pier with Caroline, watching the fireworks over the fence from Disney World.

Could I ever feel that way again with anyone else? I wondered.

"Damn right!" I told myself, standing there hugging up on a woman I was caring about and trusting more and more by the second.

I leaned over and whispered, "You're beautiful, Paige."

And I couldn't help but think about her eyes. Once I looked into her beautiful, brown eyes, all those nerves just went away. She's just got this calming personality about her. All I could think was that I was definitely going to get lost in her brown eyes every day of my life.

She'd definitely stolen my heart—I was just so excited. I was blushing and nervous and my knees were weak and I was sweating to death even though it was 45 degrees outside. It takes someone special to do that to you.

And then something totally unexpected happened—another surprise on this night of surprises: She started weeping uncontrollably—really sobbing. This wasn't the response I was hoping for in that moment. But there it was.

What I had no way of knowing was that the scandal she had endured—the release of the compromising photographs that had embarrassed her and cost her the job at NASCAR—had happened just a few months before at the start of July.

The fireworks show, as awesome as it was, reminded her of her mindset at the start of July, when she was too ashamed to leave her home to go outside and enjoy the fireworks on the Fourth of July. Here I was, trying to be romantic, and in the process I'd lit up the sky with the one thing that could emotionally take her back to the worst experience in her life. This is how it played out:

PAIGE: I know you didn't know this, like this is about to make me cry because I was fired on July first. And July Fourth was like, I was at my house crying the whole time.

BUBBA: So this is your July Fourth right now?

PAIGE: No, it's like, it's the only time of year you really have fireworks. [LAUGHS] Ugh. So I was at the house cryin' the whole time. It was like the worst week of my life. [CRIES] Well, when you think of fireworks, you think of the Fourth of July. And, uh, I was fired July first and then I had to cope with the whole world seeing these pictures of me.

PAIGE: It was the worst week of my whole life and I was in bed all day. Three days after I was fired and I didn't get to have fireworks. Ugh. Thanks.

PAIGE: (To Camera) Oh yeah, so I didn't get to see fireworks this year. Gosh. [CRIES] I did not think that was gonna happen. Who would've thought? This is such a wonderful date—love's in the air and here I am cryin' and I'm so glad it was with him. I just put my head in his chest. I didn't feel like I had to hold my emotions back with him.

PAIGE:	You have my mascara on your shirt.
BUBBA:	I don't care sweetie. It's beautiful isn't it?
PAIGE:	Yeah, it is.

She cried on and on, but I think I can honestly say what happened in that moment brought us closer together than I'd ever hoped for. She put her head on my shoulder and just let it all out.

"I'm so sorry," she kept saying.

"You're good," I said back, determined to be there for her for however long it took.

"Ugh, my makeup looks like a mess," she said, mascara washing down her cheeks.

"You look beautiful," I repeated, meaning every word.

As she told me the story of being ashamed and disgraced, of having a preacher over to help comfort her, of waking up in the mornings not wanting to see or speak to anyone, of being emotionally destroyed, that fireworks show faded off into the distance.

I knew one thing for damn sure: If Paige was with me, no one would ever hurt her again. I'd fight every day to protect her and provide for her—that's the cowboy way. I explained this that night:

BUBBA:	(To Camera) Paige is with me. There's nothing gonna happen to her. She's not gonna have to go through no heartache. I can promise you this: As long as she's with me, she'll never be upset again.

PAIGE:	[LAUGHS] Is my mascara runnin'?
BUBBA:	No, you're good. You're good.
PAIGE:	Okay.
BUBBA:	Look at that! Look at that! Look at that!
PAIGE:	(To Camera) It was the finale. Bubba is the kind of guy that makes you feel safe and secure and protected. And I know he would take care of me and I know he'll kiss the ... the tears off my cheeks when I'm crying and I know he'll take care of things and it's so easy to be with him. It would, it's perfect.
PAIGE:	I want to, like, clap [LAUGHS]. Good job.
BUBBA:	Just kiss me instead. How about that?
PAIGE:	Okay.

I came home and wedged that card she wrote me right above me on the bunk bed, underneath the box spring on the bunk above me so I could see it at night. No one had done something like that for me in a long, long time, and it felt good.

This wasn't about winning or losing for me; it wasn't a competition. It was about feeling the way I want to feel. And for the first time in a long time, I felt really good.

It was a special moment for her to share with me the most traumatic thing that had ever happened to her. It made me think about the most traumatic experience in my life, and it's a story I've never told before.

It's about the birth of my son.

6

TOUGH DECISIONS

This story begins when I was in ninth grade.

I went to a very strict, but very prominent, small Christian school.

My best times there were spent playing first base, and I was sure enough a very gifted baseball player. I hit two home runs in several games and in some I hit three over the fence in a day. It came easy to me. I still hold the record down there in Winter Garden (where I'm from) for hitting the most home runs in a season. My dad was a great athlete, and I think both of our dreams were to try to make it to the big leagues.

I was the first baseman, and I was known for never letting a ball get past me. If I needed to, I could sure enough do the splits to stretch all the way out and reach for a throw. There's no way I could do it now, but back then it was all so easy.

My dad had a little set-up for me by our house where I would practice for hours after school—a little ol' field set-up where I could throw balls and practice hitting. I couldn't get enough of it.

My best friend at the time was Augusta. I was 14, and she was 17 and really cute—blonde hair, blue eyes, very athletic. While I was at baseball practice, she was at basketball, and we would meet up after. She was super sweet and fun to be around.

We would always go to the movies or over to the wing shack, which was called Flyer's Wings, and we just hung out for hours eating wings together. We sat beside each other in history class and worked off each other's papers. We did what other teenagers did—went to the mall, rode around on three-wheelers and four-wheelers, that kind of stuff.

Never once at that time did it occur to me that we would be together. I just thought we were cool friends. It never felt like it was going to be any kind of relationship. Remember, I was 14—I didn't know the first thing about any of that stuff.

It was a given that if one of us had practice, the other would be waiting there by the locker room for the other to come out. We would just get in her car and head to the ice cream store or for more wings, and do homework and hang out. Any time I needed to talk about something, she was always there.

I had a pretty big crush on one of her close friends, Rachel, and I would go on and on about it. Then one day Augusta said, "Forget about her. Just leave Rachel alone. She isn't your style anyways. It's not gonna work."

We were sitting in the wing shack when she said it. My usual order there was 20 wings, fries, and ranch—I could eat 20 wings just like that—and I always poured vinegar all over them to make them tangier, but on this night she said to me, "Don't do that!"

"Why?" I said.

"That will make your breath stink and I don't want it stinky later."

What?

It didn't make any sense to me because I always ordered the same thing. And then the thought occurred to me that maybe she was going to kiss me.

And sure enough she did.

We left the wing place and wound up going back to my mom's place. We were sitting on the couch, watching TV like we had a million times before. But on this night, she moved closer very quickly, and before I knew it, she was on top of me kissing me and coming on to me pretty hard.

I didn't stop her. I didn't turn her down, and one thing led to the next. Truthfully I wasn't even sure what was happening.

I didn't know what to do. I'd never touched a woman like that, or even been around it. I'd never even seen it unless it was in a magazine, and I was nervous. I had no idea what was going on, and my 14-year-old mind didn't know to stop it either.

The encounter was over very quickly, and I was more confused than anything. It wasn't anything like I'd wanted that moment to be. Heck, I was 14 years old at the time; I had no idea what to expect.

But everything, everything had changed.

We'd done gone and slept together. Confused, I took a shower, and when I got out, I found her getting her clothes ready, putting her dress back on. She said quietly, "Well, okay. I'm gonna go."

I said, "Okay," not knowing what else I should say. She headed out to her car, so I walked out there behind her, and all of a sudden she starts bawling and I said, "What's the matter?"

She said to me, "It's my 14th day."

I said, "What?" I didn't know what she was talking about. I had no idea.

She said, "Fourteen."

I said, "What's that mean?"

She said, "The 14th day in between my period."

At that point I still didn't have any idea what she was trying to get at.

She said, "That's when people try to get pregnant."

And I knew right then and there that she was going to be pregnant. My heart sunk. I was standing outside of my mother's apartment at the edge of the parking lot, right there next to Augusta's purple Honda Civic when she told me all of this. I remember it clearer than day.

She was crying, and I didn't know what to think or what to do. I just knew that she was going to be pregnant.

All of this happened on a Friday, and I worried about it all weekend long. I tried to sort out in my head what had just happened and what was about to happen, but I was still lost. Monday finally came, and we were back at school, and Augusta gave me the cold shoulder the whole time. I didn't think I'd done anything wrong, and I had no idea how to handle the situation, especially at school. It went on like that for a few long weeks, and then she started telling me that we needed to talk about it.

I said, "You don't even know if you're pregnant or not. Why are we even worrying about it right now?"

She said, "Well, I am. I am pregnant."

I said, "How do you know?"

She said, "'Cause it was my 14th day."

Then I started thinking, well, maybe she just wanted to be, but I tried to put the thought out of my mind and focus on the situation. We went to a private school, and they kicked you out for going to an R-rated movie. If they found out you went to an R-rated movie or if you had Copenhagen or anything like that on you, they'd kick you clean out of that school. So I knew that if they found out we had sex, much less that she was pregnant, they were going to kick us clean out of that school without a question.

A couple months went by and Augusta wound up telling one of her friends, who was a teacher at the school, and that teacher wound up turning us in. I remember it was at the Fall Festival, and the principal or one of the pastors came up to me and said, "Come with us."

I said, "Okay."

I knew right where I was headed—to the office to get interrogated about what happened and about whether or not we'd slept together and the whole situation.

Well, they asked me.

I said, "Yep, we sure did."

It was kind of a blur to me from that moment on, but they called our parents up there. They had me go in the room and speak with her dad, and then they had my dad go in there and speak with her. Her dad was saying, "Well, you're 14 years old. What were y'all thinking?"

And I just said, "Well I don't ... I didn't know what I was doing. I didn't ... I didn't think anything was going to happen."

His response was simply, "We'll handle all this."

Augusta then had her turn to talk to my parents, and she told my dad that she was in love with me, wanted to marry me, and all this other stuff.

My dad said, "Listen, he's 14 years old. He's got his whole life ahead of him. He ain't gettin' married, you know what I mean? He's 14."

They kicked me out of school for having sex with her. Her pregnancy didn't even factor into the equation because they didn't have any idea whether or not she was pregnant at the time. That news would come a few days later—followed by the word from Augusta's family that they didn't want me to play any role in being the boy's father or being around her while she was expecting.

I was pretty much humiliated for a while because here I was: I was a Thompson, and Thompsons didn't do stupid stuff like that. I kind of hung my head down low. I had to transfer to the public school, but in small towns like mine, that news follows you everywhere.

I hurt my whole family because everyone knew. I felt so bad about how it affected my mother, which was pretty bad because, of course, it happened at her place, under her supervision, supposedly. I could care less about how I felt at the time, but I hated it for my whole family: my two older sisters, my mom, my dad, and my grandparents because I had embarrassed them.

The whole thing was so tough on me that I stayed out of baseball that season. To get my head right, my dad made me do every chore he could think of and more, and then made me do them again. He worked me hard to teach me a lesson and to punish me, but I guess more than anything it was to remind me of what I did and the consequences that come from our decisions.

I didn't know my son was born until my dad got a call, the evening after he'd been delivered. Augusta's family had taken care of all of it, and they didn't even call me—they called my dad.

I remember him slamming the phone down and saying, "Come on, let's go. We gotta go to the hospital."

I said, "What for?"

He said, "Your son's been born," and it didn't really register. I just followed him out the door. I was 15. And the next thing I knew, I was sitting there holding this baby that was mine. His name was Reid, and his eyes—goodness gracious.

My buddy, Billy, went with me. I was so nervous. I was a 15-year-old holding a child. There's something serious.

So from then on I worked after school for my dad. With what money I did make, I would go up to the Circle-K, and I would buy a money order, have it made out to her name, and send it to her. But she'd always send it back to me. She didn't want it.

I felt like I needed to provide for him. I wanted to do whatever I could, but Augusta's family would always send the money back to me. They never took it, and months later, I had stacks of these money orders in her name that I couldn't cash.

I finally was able to talk to her, and I said, "What's goin' on with this, Augusta? Why, why aren't you takin' this money for the baby and for things that you need?"

She said, "Well, I just don't want your money. I don't need your money. You hadn't been around the whole pregnancy."

I said, "You're right. I hadn't been around the whole pregnancy. Y'all told me y'all didn't want me around. What do you want me to do? Every time I turn around, I'm ... I try to do somethin' right, and you're makin' it out like I'm doin' somethin' wrong. I'll just back away. I'll just stay away until you want me to have somethin' to do with him."

Several months passed. They let my mother see him, but they wouldn't let me see him or spend any time with him. As he got a little older, I'd watch him a little bit here and there. It was a tough thing to deal with because I grew up in a split family, and I knew how hard it could be on a kid. And he was young, real young.

I just knew that he was getting old enough to be at that critical part of his life where he would realize who his mom and dad were and wonder why they didn't live together. I knew that he shouldn't have to go through that. He didn't need to go through what I went through. I didn't want to make it even harder on him so, as he got older and older, I'd see him less and less.

Augusta married a nice guy. He actually went to high school with my two older sisters, who are ten and eight years older than me. She married him, and they started a family together.

I remember being 17 or 18 and thinking how much I'd like to see Reid, but there was always turmoil. I'd go there to pick him up, after she said I could take him to Chuck E. Cheese, and she'd say, "No. I changed my mind."

He'd say something to her and she'd change her mind. It wasn't healthy for Reid to be seeing this stuff, much less to be mixed up in the middle of it. Half the time he wouldn't want to go with me because he'd be confused, wondering why a stranger was coming to pick him up. It was tough to hear that, but it also made me realize what I had to do. I made the decision to put his needs, and his mom's needs, ahead of mine.

I just knew that it would be better for him to be with his mother and a stable father figure. He had a brother and sister already, and it wasn't right for me to mix all of that up. People can say what they want to about the situation, but I don't care because until you're growing up in that situation and go through it and understand what I was facing, you will never understand the pain and confusion.

Either way, it's just rough on a kid. But I knew he could have a stable family and that he would still know that I'm his dad. I couldn't stop him from having that. For him to have a good life, this was what he needed. I was still a kid myself, so I stepped away for a long time. I knew I'd be okay eventually, but I knew I had to give it some time.

Walking away from that situation was one of the hardest things I've ever had to do because I have a son, and everybody knows that he's mine, and everybody's going to know that I stepped away and that I don't keep in contact, especially in a small town. Everyone is going to make their judgments.

But I had to because it wasn't fair for him to have to bounce back and forth between me and Augusta and for him to lie in bed at night wondering, "Why do I have two daddies and why is my mama not with this guy?" I had to keep reminding myself of that. I didn't want stuff that was going through my head as a child going through his head. I had to make it better for him in any way that I could. He didn't deserve any less.

I think of him every day. Not a day has gone by when I haven't thought and prayed about him. As he got a little older, I was super proud to learn he was an athlete in prep school just like me.

The little things, the daily things, were some of the hardest to deal with. It was hard not going to his games. They never even told me when the games were. I'd ask for a schedule, but they wouldn't give me a schedule. I could've gone out of my way and just shown up, but I didn't want to go where I wasn't wanted.

And I didn't want to show up there and have him see me and get his mind off what he's supposed to be doing; when you're an athlete, you're supposed to be tuned in on your game. You're not supposed to be distracted and worrying, and that kind of goes back to me not wanting to mess with his heart and his mind.

My buddies at the time were some of the people that helped me get through it the most. They would always call me and tell me, "Hey, man. Your son's just like you. He caught the first catch today, returned the kick off, ran all the way back," or "He hit a couple balls out of the park today," I kept up with his sports through my buddies because a lot of them had little brothers, or they would coach and go watch the games.

It would make me very proud every time I heard one of their stories. It made me feel great because I could say, "Yeah, well he should, you know, it's bred into him! Heck yeah!" It would put a smile on my face to know that he was doing well. But it was heartbreaking at the same time, to tell you the honest truth.

He was a bleach-blonde-headed, blue-eyed, cute little boy, built just like me. He was just a good-looking little ole kid.

When Reid was 13, Augusta and his family moved to Alabama for a while. They actually lived across the street, through the woods, in a log cabin.

Reid would come up to the house every day and visit me for a little while, and then he would go hang out with Colton, my nephew, because they're right at the same age, and they would play. For a while things seemed good.

We got to spend a lot of time together. We'd go shopping and he'd go with me to the arena, and then he'd go with me to work. He started riding horses and things like that.

Everywhere I went, people would tell me they all thought he was my little brother. Well, he started spending a little less time with his mom and her family and a lot more time with me. Quickly though, they nipped that in the bud. They didn't like it, so it went back to the old way: I had to ask permission and we were having the back-and-forth conversation about him in front of him.

"Can Reid go with me here?"

"Well, no. He's got somethin' to do tonight with so-and-so."

I'd gotten his attention. He was really starting to spend a lot of time with me and they didn't like it. Things started getting uncomfortable again.

One day we were going to Dothan. I was going to get the kid some jeans because he was growing out of the pair he had on. We were riding down the road in silence. I was driving on State Road 52 in between Malvern and Taylor, coming into Dothan. I still remember right where I was. It was right past the produce stand. We had just passed it, and we were coming up to the red light in Taylor. The brakes of the truck finished squealing, and the wind noise from the windows quieted down for a moment. It was a cold, rainy, dreary day right before Christmas.

We came up to the stoplight there, and he just looked over at me and he said, "Daddy, I remember you coming to pick me up when I was little."

I said, "You do?"

He said, "Yeah."

He said, "I also remember Mom not letting me go with you."

I didn't say a word.

And right then, I knew that he was getting older; he was maturing; he was starting to figure things out. And I knew it was hard for him to say that. I also knew that it meant a few things. I knew right then and there that later on down the road he would want to spend more time with me. It was a wonderful thing for him to say, and it's given me a world of peace of mind, knowing someday that's a possibility for us. He understood the way things had worked as he was growing up.

I knew that he was mine, and he knew I was his dad and that he has another dad too that takes care of him. He was smart enough even then to know that there were two of us, and that when the time was right, he could come back around and we would find a way to be father and son.

That's my prayer.

Being a father has affected me. I've had to mature a lot faster, especially because this all started when I was 14, 15 years old. I didn't go out and party a lot like most of my other friends did. I very well could have, but I didn't because I had a son and I didn't want to be the guy everyone talked about around town. "Oh, well he's got this son. He's a deadbeat dad, but he's over here running these parties all night long and doing this."

I think about him all the time when I'm out there riding. I often wish that he was with me. I think that he needs to be around me, and I think he needs to learn the things that I know. My dad taught me everything that I know—my dad and my grandfather. They taught me about building things, how to treat people, how to dress, how to treat others with respect. I can tell he's learning these things, but it's still hard to know he's learning them from someone else.

Many times I comfort myself by thinking this is part of a higher plan. And among the many blessings I have in life is that his mom and her husband are wonderful people at heart. I know they're raising him well to be a true Southern gentleman.

He could come back as a young adult and say, "Yes, sir. No, sir," to me and listen to me, and want to respect me. Or he could be the complete opposite and just resent me for never being around. I don't want that to be the case.

A lot of times I'll be riding in the pasture, and I speak to him through prayer and tell him that I love him and that I wish I could be around him, but I know that I can't.

It has taught me that you can love deeply, even if it is from far away. It matured me a lot, and, more than anything, it's taught me what I need to do when I do get married and have more children. My son has opened my eyes in an unexpected way, and I hope to teach him as much as his presence in my life has taught me about how to be a real cowboy.

7

Cowboy Up

By now there were only a handful of us left, and the group was pretty evenly split between us guys from the country and a few of the "city boys" here to impress Paige with their talk about bright lights and a life of glamour in the concrete jungle.

A bunch of them took her down on a private plane to Miami, and it left the country guys cooped up and going out of our minds with nothing to do except be bored and jealous at the same time.

While they were in Miami, those guys took her out in a Ferrari, on a speedboat designed by Porsche, to hotel penthouses and expensive restaurants. It got a lot of us thinking about our lifestyle versus theirs, what that really meant, and whether we were jealous of them spending time with Paige or whether there was a twang of jealousy in us that maybe guys like that could provide her with something we couldn't.

After all, my life is pretty clearly defined. I'm at home in pastures, doctoring cattle, living off the land, and doing whatever needs to be done to get the job done. I always have to be doing something productive. Personally I'll take a nice cold beer over champagne and freaking caviar any time.

My instincts told me Paige felt the same way.

When she got home, she took the remaining country guys out to a field, and we set up some targets and broke out the shotguns and rifles and spent a few hours just firing away at bottles and jars. We sent up some skeet targets too.

A beautiful woman and a Smith and Wesson go together just perfectly, in my eyes. Oh and then there's one more thing—the camo. Paige was wearing camo.

That camouflage just gets me going! Cowgirl boots! Damn! I couldn't help myself, and I went to sleep thinking about her for sure. I'd crawl through six miles of broken glass just to kiss her again.

By this time I was daydreaming about her all day long—working on the ranch together, getting done in the afternoon, crawling off the back of our horses, and before we'd load them up in the trailer just stepping off them and turning them loose in the pasture to let them graze.

The only thing I could think about was coming home after a day like that and wrapping my arms around her and kissing her until the sun set. That was the way I wanted to spend my afternoons with Paige. And after we had our little romantic afternoon and loaded everything up, then we'd just go straight back to the house and do the same thing over and over, you know?

I'm ready to be settled down and have a nice wife. If anything, the experience I was having on *Sweet Home Alabama* was reminding me of that every moment.

How could I not smile just thinking about it? I want to tell you something: That girl had my blood flowing and none of the wonderful quotes that were flying off my lips into a nearby microphone or camera were bull crap in the least.

I'd been bred to be tough and rugged, but Paige was bringing the sweet, sensitive side out. I'm a steel-coated marshmallow: I'm covered in steel but inside I'm just as soft and fluffy and sweet as a marshmallow—that's how it felt to be around Paige.

My heart had been through a lot. There was no prying or getting into it. It was closed off to everybody. Then that date on horseback on the beach turned me into a steel-coated marshmallow. I was daydreaming about her for sure. But then again, so were seven other guys—*living right there with me in the same house.*

Life in that house had taken a different toll on everyone, and the close quarters and heated emotions were bringing out the best and worst in everyone.

Remember big Shaun Bigos from New York with the hairspray trigger finger? When Shaun first walked in the door and I saw his lanky Cro-Magnon head and heard his Lurch-like voice, I thought, *I'm not going to get along with this son-of-a-buck at all.* He was running around calling us hillbillies, and I was getting ready to jack his jaw. I'm telling you, I cannot stand that for a second.

> SHAUN B: (To Camera) I can't understand a word some of these country boys say, so someone definitely needs to order me a Rosetta Stone hillbilly edition as soon as possible. Paige has got a very sexy accent. I just like that a lot. On a female, it's real sexy. On a male, it just sounds dumb. So I find that interesting.

Well, the strangest thing happened along the way. I became great friends with Shaun Bigos. He really came around.

He kind of spent the better part of two weeks mocking me and the guys for throwing our ropes around a pretend steer for hours on end. One afternoon I was practicing my roping out in the yard, and it finally got the best of him—he walked over and asked for some pointers.

He's about six foot five, and he got that loop up and swinging around his shellacked head, and he actually got pretty good at it. After a few tries we had him choking on the pretend steer pretty good. He would rope one horn and I would swing out wide and loop the other.

But it wasn't his roping that made me respect him. In the end, Shaun Bigos has a cowboy quality that any Southerner can learn from: He is, first and foremost, straightforward. He doesn't beat around the bush with you. You might not love what he has to say, but he says what he means and he's ready to back it up. Being a straight shooter is a major part of the Cowboy Code.

At one point he was ready to give up on Paige, knowing that they were from two drastically different worlds. Being here was all a joke to him; he was just here to rile all us Southern boys up and ruin our party. But then one day she got him alone, out there on the Louisiana bayou.

She made him change out of his blazer and boots and into a full outfit of camo—head to toe and rubber boots. They went off into the swamps and saw bald eagles flying overhead. They drank red wine from the bottle while the airboat skimmed over lily pads and bamboo shoots.

At one point the guy reached into the water and pulled out a live gator, and the closest this guy had ever been to a gator skin was walking by one of those fancy stores in the middle of New York.

And then he kissed her when the sun was going down in that swamp. He came back to that house giddy as the rest of us. I'm surprised he wasn't saying "y'all" by the time that date was done.

I'd hear him say, "I'm not sure whether I'm falling for Paige or falling for the South."

Having said all that, I'm convinced Paige doesn't want a man that has more damn facial creams and more bath salts than she does, you know? He's going to need a bigger countertop in the bathroom to hold all his feminine supplies than she does!

But this cowboy has a lot of respect for him.

One thing about the South—it has a way of working its magic on you. It might have even saved Shaun Bigos' life. (Turn to the end of the book for an update on his life—it's an amazing story!)

If the fight for a woman's love was having a positive effect on most of us, it was taking its toll on one of the handful of guys left in there—a farmer from Minnesota named Jeremiah Korfe.

Jeremiah was, in my opinion, a little rough around the edges and shifty to begin with. We all felt like brothers in that house, but Jeremiah was the distant one for some reason. He'd come back from his dates with Paige and seem to be an emotional wreck. One time he came back all out of sorts because she told him she had major feelings for him, and he froze up and didn't know what to say in return. He just headed to his bunk and curled up all anxious and depressed.

On another night, after some whiskey, he got all out of sorts with one of the other guys we all loved, and out of the blue he came lunging at him in the kitchen, flailing away, throwing punches and shoving at him. There was a lot of lip flapping in that house and sure enough there were people who rode up on my nerves pretty hard, but Jeremiah was the only one to raise up his fists and try to swing at someone.

The guy he swung at was one of our favorites, a fellow cowboy named Shaun Smith. Ol' Shaun is young and fearless, a calf-roper from Arkansas. Just before coming to Alabama, his horse (he'd named him "Credit Card," as in, "Don't leave home without it") had gone missing in a major theft where several prized horses had been kidnapped. A couple days before this incident with Jeremiah, his dad called to say the horse had turned up. Tragically though, the group that stole him had let him starve to death. They tied him up and didn't feed him.

Watching Shaun get the news he'd feared was heartbreaking for us all. We all came together and bowed our heads and prayed together. I think it was a blessing that he was surrounded by new friends, friends who could understand the pain of losing your horse is like losing a true loved one, friend, and partner.

It was another divide between city and country. The city boys learned something that day too: They learned about a bond a man can have with his horse. And they learned that cowboys are not afraid to cry. There were many tears shed in that house over Credit Card, and I mourn his loss with Shaun to this day.

So when Jeremiah lunged at Shaun for who knows what reason, he was taking a run at a fellow cowboy. He would later blame the people in the editing room for making it look like he was out of control, overly moping, and too aggressive when he took a swing at Shaun, which brings me to another trait that's at the very core of the Cowboy Code—knowing how to "cowboy up."

"Cowboy up" is just an old term you hear thrown around quite a bit. When somebody would get hurt—bucked off a bull, thrown off a horse, stomped on, get the rope caught around a hand—it's just something we all say to each other. When you get hurt out in the pasture, your first reaction is to say some bad words 'cause you're really hurting and in pain.

But before you can do that, if somebody says "cowboy up" to you, it just makes you forget all the pain and get back to work. It's just to remind you of who you are. It's either cowboy up or lie there and bleed. Lying there and bleeding isn't going to help you get anything done.

How does that apply to some of the things I was seeing from Jeremiah? That's an easy one, and I see it in a lot of guys.

First off, his feelings. Sure, it hurts or makes you feel vulnerable to put yourself out there—but cowboy up! Pull your skirt up, put your man pants back on. All I can say is you've got to fight for what you want. Get to the front of the line. If it means bumping elbows or knocking heads a little—meet that lady, really connect with her, talk to her, be honest, and show her that you're here for her and her only.

Wake up, buck up, grab a hold of the reins, and go forward.

I know a lot of men have been hurt before, and Jeremiah may be one of them, and he may have his reasons for acting the way he did. But guys like Jeremiah, they need to cowboy up and not be afraid to get in there.

A second way he needed to cowboy up was when it came to taking responsibility for his actions. A cowboy always does that. There are no exceptions.

You'll never hear a real cowboy pass the buck—especially after he knows he screwed up. You have a few too many and you take a swing at someone when you shouldn't have—that's the type of mess a cowboy can get himself into every now and again. I don't claim to be perfect, and there's plenty of times when I haven't walked the straight line the way I should have. But the way you can tell a true cowboy is by the way he approaches getting himself out of a jam.

Blaming someone else, whether it's the guy you're riding next to, or the dog that ate your homework, or the editors who are putting you on TV, is not taking the high road. And a cowboy is always supposed to look for the high road.

Anyway, it was down to a handful of us, and the competition for Paige was only getting stronger by the hour. Word came down that

I was going to have another day to spend with her. For sure my heart was going to be out there.

I'm always ready to cowboy up!

8

The Women Who Raise You

I might spend the bulk of my days by the backside of a cow or scrubbing out a stall, but there's one major fact of life that did not escape this cowboy by a long shot:

Women love shoes.

And here in the South that means only one thing. You want to see her smile? Go with her and pick out a new pair of boots! There's nothing like the sight of a woman in boots.

You can line up all the fancy dresses from the Academy Awards from Baldwin County to Hollywood Boulevard, but I'm telling you a pair of boots and those cut-off jeans and I am done.

And you girls know it too!

This brings me to my date with Paige, which started at the local boot store on Alabama Route 98.

BUBBA: Hey Darlin', how are you?

PAIGE: So excited.

BUBBA: You should be.

PAIGE: I am. Nothing makes me happier than cowboy boots. All right, my gosh, I'm like in heaven. Carousing Old Gringos! [LAUGHING]

BUBBA: I know, right.

PAIGE: I'm not a high-heel girl. I'm not a pocketbook girl. I spend all my money on cowboy boots. This is fun.

BUBBA: Do you like the square toe or the snip toe? That's a snip toe (I said, pointing to a pair).

PAIGE: Yes.

BUBBA: You gotta have something square toed to ride in when we go back to the ranch.

PAIGE: I know. I got some. Some oxfords, yeah, some Justin.

PAIGE: (To Camera) Bubba makes me feel so happy. He makes me feel like a woman, like a lady.

PAIGE: I want these.

BUBBA: (To Camera) Walking around the store with Paige just feels great, you know? My shoulders are bowed up. I'm ready to take on the world with her.

She finally settled on a pair of snip-toed Old Gringos. You know you're smitten when an hour goes by and you've been watching a girl try on boots, and you don't want it to end.

PAIGE: I gotta get you to help me with something else, too.

BUBBA: What's that?

PAIGE: I got me a hat and it looks stupid, and it needs shaping.

Every face has a shape and a hat should be custom shaped to fit it. Her face is full and her smile so bright, I wanted the rims to be set back as far as possible, so the brim would only slightly shield her eyes.

BUBBA: Let's get it done.

BUBBA: (To Camera) I've actually never shaped a hat for a woman, and she's the first, and she's gonna be the last.

BUBBA: You look really good in that hat, too.

PAIGE: It's too new, though.

BUBBA: Okay, we'll have to flatten it out a little bit.

PAIGE: Make it like yours 'cause yours looks good on you.

BUBBA: You are good-looking, Paige, you know that? You really are.

I put that hat on her head, but I had to look at how her face was shaped first so I could see how I wanted to make it. I didn't know if I wanted to make it punchy or ranchy or just make it kind of rodeo style. But she's just an all-around girl, so I tried to shape it like all-around cowgirl style—pitched up on the sides and pulled down in the front. She can wear that thing 24/7 and I'll be happy.

I found myself always looking for her eyes. I didn't want the brim of a hat getting in my way, but there was a flirtatiousness with how she would raise and lower that hat. When she tilted her head to the side and gave you that look from underneath, not a word needed to be said out loud.

There were a few of those little looks she gave me right there in that store that made me start thinking about the future. Right there in a shoe store looking around at all those boots.

Is there any way we will be together long enough for me to see her wear through dozens and dozens of these boots ... for years and years ...

And then another thought, as we walked up to the front to pay for them and passed the cute little aisle of tiny cowgirl boots in pink ...

Our little girl would look adorable in those someday.

What? Where is this coming from? Don't get bucked off ... stay cool ... stay in the seat ...

I slid the newly steamed hat on her head, tilted her head to one side and mine to the other so our hats could intertwine, and gave her a nice soft kiss.

PAIGE: I know. I spend all my money on boots, which are way more expensive than high heels.

BUBBA: I got a big closet at home that will fit all your stuff.

PAIGE: You do? Okay.

PAIGE: (To Camera) Bubba's ranch is already ready for me to move into. He has my own closet that will hold all my cowboy boots—and that's very important to me. That's mandatory. For a girl. We cannot share closets. There's something manly about him and just his personality and how, I guess, tough he is but how sweet he is at the same time.

PAIGE: [LAUGHING] Push it down.

BUBBA: Beautiful.

PAIGE: Does it look good?

BUBBA: Yeah. The hat looks pretty good.

PAIGE: Do I need to push it out at the top to look like yours?

BUBBA: No.

PAIGE: Looks good like it is?

BUBBA: Mm-hmm. It does. The hat looks good, but you look better.

PAIGE: Thanks.

I had a great date planned and this was just the start.

BUBBA: (To Camera) She melts this cowboy. She absolutely does. She really does. I mean, she's absolutely amazing.

I told Paige I was going to see her in a couple hours, and I was headed off to fix her something for lunch.

I love to cook. It calms me down and relaxes my mind. It also fills my mind with great memories from growing up and learning from my mom and my sisters.

I got us a place at an historic Victorian home in Mobile called the Fort Conde Inn. It's a classic Southern mansion with an iron gate, flowered walkway, massive white pillars, and smooth heart-pine floors. The stairways and moldings are all custom milled. The chandeliers are spotless crystal.

It got me thinking about my own home and how I wished I had the time and resources to make a place like this someday. As someone who has built a home from the ground up, I can tell you some truly gifted people put a lot of work into making this a special place, that's for sure.

It felt like something right out of *Gone with the Wind*, only this place had an industrial-sized kitchen! And I was all ready to get to work. I had a side of ribs and some spices, French-style green beans, and a broccoli casserole all laid out and ready to go.

The quickest way to a woman's heart is through her belly, so that's where I headed. I got some broccoli casserole that I learned from my older sister, and the country-style ribs, and throw that little Southern hospitality in there 'cause everybody's gotta have a rib every once in a while. I used a little seasoning that I mixed up myself—I like to call it Bubba's butt rub.

Like I said, my mom and my sisters taught me how to cook. And as I slid the braised ribs in and started to smell them coming to life and filling this wonderful home, I got to thinking that these very strong women in my life also taught me a lot about how a woman should be treated.

My sisters always had boyfriends here and there when I was growing up. I was much younger than they were, but I could see what was going on with them all the time.

We lived in a modest two-story home near the orange groves, and the windows were always open, especially in the summertime. You could always smell the fruit growing in the pasture, and you could always get a sense of what was going on with your family under that roof.

Sometimes they'd be upset about something and I would think, *Golly, I'd never do that or I'd never be mean to her.* There was no sense to it half the time, and there's no way I'd ever want to make someone feel the way my sisters were feeling. I mean, women are tenderhearted people—most of 'em are anyway. Some of them are tough, but they're still tender and you have to treat them with respect—even when they aren't treating you with respect or when they don't like you.

My sister Lara is the super-sensitive type. She'd been in love with the same guy since practically the second grade. Then came the day they had to set off to go to college in different places. It hurt her so bad and then he sent word he was seeing another girl there.

Our bedrooms were close to each other upstairs, and I just remember her never, ever coming out of her room for days. She would dash out real quick and get some food and then scurry right back up the steps and slam the door behind her. I remember all those nights sitting in bed and hearing through the windows the sound of her crying on and on. I knew I never wanted to make anyone feel that way in my life.

It killed her to know he was off with someone else when she was still so madly in love with him. A couple years went by and I saw him back in town, and man, I just wanted to deck him right there for the toll he had taken on her. Of course, I'd never do that to somebody.

But it made a big impression on me. Seeing my sister dealing with heartbreak made me vow to treat a woman's feelings and her heart as something sacred.

When I was on the verge of doing something wrong, Lara would be the one to say to me, "Now Bubba, that's not nice" or "You shouldn't do anything like that," and that's all it would take to keep me on the right path.

Eventually she forgave that boy from second grade she had the crush on and fell in love with. In fact, she more than forgave him—she married him! And I cried like a baby at their wedding. They're wonderful people living a wonderful love story.

Lara is the sensitive one and my sister Lisa is the one with thicker skin. She and I clash heads from time to time, but hey, who doesn't have a sibling like that? She's the one I always turn to when I need to hear it how it is. She holds nothing back; she's the strong one. I get a lot of the cowboy toughness from her and it, too, has served me very well over the years. The balance of these two traits, sensitive and tough, is the product of the wonderful combination that is my mother Lana.

My mom is the sweetest lady and she lives right next door to me to this day. She's had a tough life, and she defines what it means to be a true and strong and prideful Southern woman.

I was seven and in second grade the day it all happened. It's still one of those days that lives on in my mind in slow motion.

My momma came and picked me up from school that day. She cried all the way back to the house, and I kept saying, "What's wrong, Momma? What's wrong?"

She said, "Nothin' honey, nothin'."

When I got home, everyone, including Lara and Lisa, were sitting at the big dinner table. My mom and dad were standing there, and they told me to sit down.

My sisters were already in tears. My dad had a beard at the time—I remember that distinctly—and he said, "Son and girls, your mom and I are gonna get a divorce."

Lara and Lisa busted out crying all over again, but I didn't know what a divorce was. I was like, "What is that? What do you mean?"

And Lisa, who has a way of just cutting right to it, said, "That means they're not gonna be together, Bubba!"

So, okay, huh.

I said, "What are we gonna do?"

And Dad said, "You're gonna stay with your momma for a while."

"Okay, well, are you comin' too?"

You know, I didn't know. I just didn't know what was going on.

I think you can make the argument that the day your parents tell you they are splitting up is the last official day of your childhood. For me it was at age seven. I remember a bunch of us all sitting there in tears. Dad was crying and saying he was so sorry to all of us. Everyone was just upset, and the next thing you know he's moving out, and we're moving to a new place.

There are years after that that are a complete blur.

But the thing I remember most was how I hated to see my mother upset. I still do to this day. She's the sweetest lady in the world, and she has faced some awful pain in her life. I get so mad all the time because how can someone so sweet have so much nonsense going on around her all the time?

People will sometimes say to me, "You're so sweet, Bubba. Why are you like that? What are you after?"

And I'm like, "I'm not after anything."

I come from a house full of women. I just think that this world would be a better place if men respected women more than they do. And, you know? I'm the only Thompson here to carry on my name, but the women around me shaped my life in a major way.

And they taught me how to cook!

Thompson Family Photo Album

(Left): As a kid, if I wasn't in school, you were likely to find me on the baseball diamond. (Right): And if I wasn't playing baseball, I was probably with my grandfather, learning some of the greatest lessons in a man's life, like how to saddle up!

Three generations of Thompsons on the porch.

Sometimes you can't beat growing up with family on a ranch.

Lake Sawyer, home to many of my greatest memories.

Me and my sisters Lisa (left) and Laura (right).

The most important woman in my life, my mom Lana.

*Arriving on the ranch during the filming of "Sweet Home Alabama"
sitting with a group of guys I would come to know
as great friends of mine.*

*Sunset on the beach with Paige, still one of the most beautiful
dates I have had the privilege of sharing with anyone.*

One of the many great and unexpected things to come of the Sweet Home Alabama experience was all of the people I got to meet after the show that I would have never known otherwise. So many new supporters and friends.

Spending my time in the barn, as usual.
Life on the ranch never gets old when you love what you do!

9

LIVING BY YOUR WORD

The country-style ribs were halfway done when Paige walked up the brick path leading into the mansion, her hat perfectly shaped.

BUBBA: Hey, darlin'.

PAIGE: (To Camera) And this handsome cowboy is waiting at the front door for me, and gives me a big hug and a kiss and leads me in. As soon as I walk in, I'm just hit by the whiff of this delicious-smelling food.

PAIGE: I'm so excited. Oh, it smells good.

BUBBA: I'm gonna stir this up real quick.

PAIGE: What you cooking?

BUBBA: Some country-style ribs, you know?

PAIGE: Ummm, that looks good.

PAIGE: (To Camera) It just blows my mind
             that he does everything he does. Um,
             you know, at my house, us girls do the
             cooking in the kitchen, and my daddy
             grills. Bubba does it all. He takes care
             of everything and everybody.

BUBBA: That's got a little while to cook, so
             let's go upstairs and have a glass of
             champagne.

PAIGE: Okay.

We sat on the second-story porch and looked out onto the gas-lamp lined cobblestone street. It was quiet and the right moment to tell her exactly how I was feeling.

BUBBA: We got a lot of stuff ... excuse me
             ... we got a lot of stuff in common,
             you know? You get me mixed up by
             the way! I don't get nervous about
             nothing.

PAIGE: Nothing?

BUBBA: Nothing. I mean nothing. But uh,
             you know, I have feelings for you,
             Paige, you know? I'm not gonna beat
             around the bush and tell you that I
             don't because ...

PAIGE: I don't want you to.

BUBBA: You know, you've had to do that, you've had to deal with that your whole life, and I've had to deal with that from other people too, you know? So just straight to the point, I do care about you.

PAIGE: And I care for you, too, and I was so happy to see ... you make everything feel better. You make me not worry about everything. I feel like everything's gonna be taken care of with you. I feel like I can trust you, and like, you're honestly one of the best guys I've ever met in my whole life.

BUBBA: Well, Paige, I'll always protect you and stand up for whatever you want to do and back you 100 percent. That's just the type of man I am, so whether it's you picking me or you picking the next guy, I want you to do what's best for you.

PAIGE: Thanks, Bubba. Thank you for telling me that, too.

PAIGE: (To Camera) When I was sitting on the porch with Bubba, I just felt so special. I'm so thankful the Lord brought this guy into my life. He's so wonderful, he's so sweet, and he's so caring, and you can just look in his eyes and tell how wonderful of a soul this guy has.

PAIGE: You're like one of the best persons I've really ever met—the best guys I've ever met.

BUBBA: Well I ... I ... I can say the same about you.

PAIGE: Thanks.

BUBBA: And uh, it's been tough the last couple nights trying to go to sleep 'cause I lay there in the bed thinking about you. That card you gave me, it's uh, I'm on the bottom bunk and it's stuck in between the bars.

PAIGE: You're so funny. Tell me about your ranch at home. How do you have an extra closet already?

BUBBA: About three years ago, I started building my house. I drew it up on a piece of notebook paper. I lived in it for a year and a half with no flooring—just concrete—and I lived in it for almost two years with no kitchen. In my laundry room I had a little sink in there.

PAIGE: Okay.

BUBBA: And then I had a stove in the kitchen, so I cooked, you know?

PAIGE: A refrigerator.

BUBBA: I lived off of Vienna sausages and ramen noodles for I don't know how long, but ...

PAIGE: Beanie weenies.

BUBBA: But you know, I was just constantly saving money, putting money into the house. And I'm really proud of it.

PAIGE: I bet it's hard.

BUBBA: You know, I built it to ... to find somebody to fall in love with, to get married, and have kids, you know? It's a five-bedroom but I made one room.

PAIGE: Really?

BUBBA: I made one room a big, long room, so it's actually a four-bedroom, three bath. And it's got his and hers sinks. And a jacuzzi tub, stuff like that, you know? I mean I went all out on it, and everything in the house I did— the tile throughout the house, I hand chiseled the edges. I mean, just a lot of craftsmanship.

PAIGE: Yeah. I want to see it. I bet it's so pretty.

BUBBA: You will. You will. I'm really proud of it, and I think I did pretty good decorating it.

PAIGE: That's probably so.

BUBBA: I mean, not a lot of decorations in it. A lot of deer heads.

PAIGE: Yes, which is important.

BUBBA: Yeah, very good, nice-sized bucks.

PAIGE: I have my antlers we can put up. No heads.

BUBBA: Awesome.

PAIGE: I haven't shot a good enough one yet. I might just give you the antlers.

PAIGE: (To Camera) I could easily imagine myself sitting on Bubba's ranch on his front porch, watching the sun set, sitting there and talking and just feeling so in love and living happily ever after. It would be so easy, and it's what I've always dreamed about.

BUBBA: I probably ought to go check on the food.

PAIGE: 'kay. Smells good.

BUBBA: I don't want to burn it.

PAIGE: No, that would be ...

BUBBA: That would be a train wreck.

PAIGE: Yes. Be almost a deal breaker. Be like, oh ...

BUBBA: Good date, gone bad.

BUBBA: (To Camera) Paige makes me feel all crazy inside, you know? I mean, I don't know what she does to me— she just makes me feel real good. I mean, she brings out the sensitive side in this old cowboy here.

BUBBA: You sit right there, and I'm gonna go make the plate for you, okay?

We sat down at the table in the formal dining room and removed our hats.

Saying grace before the meal is part of the Cowboy Code of being grateful for everything you have. We always pray before we eat because the Lord's the reason why we have food to eat. He made everything that you see right now, and it's something to be thankful for because there are so many people in the world that don't have anything to be thankful for.

Saying grace is a way to be thankful to Him and to also be respectful to those who are not as fortunate. And all it takes is a few little words. So we always say grace and say a prayer before our meal, thanking Him for the food that we're about to put in our bodies.

A good way to see if someone is in touch with their spiritual side is to just take a moment at the table before you eat and lower your head for a moment. I put down in front of Paige a full plate of country-style ribs and green beans, with steam rising from the plate and the Bubba's butt rub seasoning in the air.

I do think it's an important quality—believing in God or having a religion, whatever it might be they believe in. That kind of shows that they'll bow to somebody, that they know that they're not the highest man on the totem pole, so to speak, that there's somebody greater than them and they have a sense of humility.

And I just loved it when Paige asked to say grace.

PAIGE: Should be tasty enough, huh? You want to say a blessing?

BUBBA: I will. Absolutely. Dear Heavenly Father, we come to you today, Lord, and I just want to thank you for this opportunity to be with a beautiful young lady like Paige, Lord. I pray that you bless us whichever way we're supposed to go. Guide our footsteps and keep us safe. Amen.

PAIGE: Amen. Thank you.

BUBBA: (To Camera) You know, before the meal, you always need to say grace because if it wasn't for the good man above, we wouldn't have anything. And Paige is a good, spiritual woman, you know? She believes in God, and that's just the right thing to do.

PAIGE: What do you like to do for fun?

BUBBA: I like to train colts.

PAIGE: Uh-huh. You do? Do you ... is that part of your business?

BUBBA: It's not part of my business. It's just a hobby of mine.

PAIGE: Okay, I didn't know if you took them in.

BUBBA: Like if I get a really nice horse, I'll train him myself.

PAIGE: Okay. You like to break them?

BUBBA: Mm-hmm.

PAIGE: You do.

BUBBA: Yeah, I like the first ... I like the first five rides.

PAIGE: Okay.

BUBBA: I like it when they're bucking.

PAIGE: Yeah, me too, obviously.

BUBBA: When they start listening, I don't care anymore.

PAIGE: You just send them off? This is so
            good.

BUBBA: Thank you.

PAIGE: (To Camera) It was delicious. And
            it's the best meal I've had in a long
            time. And that says a lot about a guy.
            He cooks it, he prepares it, he gets
            it ready, and he can ... he can do
            everything.

PAIGE: I wanna be able to take care of
            myself, but I want someone to take
            care of me if that makes any sense.

When we kissed on the balcony of that historic Southern mansion that day, I was sure of only one thing.

I had fallen in love.

But for now, with other guys still in the picture, I wasn't ready to say it out loud. This was a wonderful feeling. But it was scary too. I was filled with confidence. When you get back from being with a wonderful woman who is lighting up your world, you can't wait to tell your roommates all about it. But when your roommates are in love with her too, that's a big problem.

It's only natural to want to talk to the people around you about the important things going on in your life. I came home from that date with Paige on cloud nine. I mean, all the other guys could see it all over my face—there was no sense in hiding it. But lately I've been thinking about the value of not sharing your relationship status with other people around you. All day long is seems like we're all bombarded with messages, posts, updates, feeds with everyone's business being spread all over the place. Where I grew up, your feed was the corn mash you fed to the cattle—hay, straw,

grains, and so⟩ ·by-
moment, play for
lunch.

Facebook and Twitter are bringing an element to everyone that's really rooted in small-town life: These days everybody seems to know everybody's business. And my point is, especially when it comes to relationships, that isn't always a good thing.

What's going on between two people, whether it's falling in love or falling out of love, should stay between those people; it should be as private as possible. I'm not talking about reaching out for help when you need it—we all need a shoulder to lean on or the advice of a close friend. There's no greater comfort in the world.

But in general we live in a world where people shoot their mouths first and ask questions later. And when it comes to your relationship, my advice is, trust your own instincts—not the advice of the town choir—and keep it as quiet as possible. The thing about a small town is that everybody knows your business before you do. They really do. You've stepped in a puddle of mud on this side of the street and by the time you get across the street, you're covered in mud, and everyone knows all about it.

A small-town sense of pride—there's nothing like it. Small-town values and hospitality—they're some of the best parts of a good Southern life. But small-town gossip? It's just toxic.

And there's an infinite supply.

I think gossip like this hurts the relationship because if you and this girl are having a relationship and you start involving your friends and asking their opinions, and if she's doing the same thing, well, it's like the pyramid thing.

It starts off small up here at the top, but as it grows, it gets bigger and bigger and bigger because their friends have now talked to

thei   ınd the stories
alwa

I thi   small towns,
or e   f privacy. The
distc   ajor issues for
relationships. It happens all the time, especially in small towns. It
spreads unbelievably fast, and once it's out there, you'll never get
it back.

It seems like some people's idea of fun is wrecking reputations and
taking other people's problems and using them for entertainment. I
think a lot of people back in this small town talk a lot of gossip and
make things up about other people because they're so aggravated
and upset about the choices they've made in their own lives. They
feel like they have to talk about somebody else to make themselves
feel better about their own decisions.

So at the end of the day, I guess being in a small town has taught
me that for a good relationship to function, you're best keeping the
details of the thing to yourself. The relationship is meant to be had
between the two people that are in it, not between every member
of the town. No relationship has ever been saved by small-town
gossip, but many millions have been wrecked by it.

These days, thanks to Facebook and Twitter, there are no real
secrets. We all live in a small town when it comes to gossip. My
advice is to find a real friend you can trust or turn to—not the
318 "friends" you have on Facebook or the 273 followers you
have on Twitter. And if someone comes to you for help, or shares
something near and dear, then you best keep your mouth sealed.

Giving someone your word, and living by that word, is a major
part of the Cowboy Code. When you pass along a piece of gossip,
you're wounding someone's heart. The same thing applies to
handling disputes in your own life. In disputes, drama is your
enemy. Nothing good ever comes of it. Most of the time when

I have a dispute with somebody, I go straight to them. A good example is a little dust-up that happened not too long ago.

We had a dispute with James, a man that we buy feed from. Jack, our business partner, had to go out of town to have surgery on his back. James happens to know a man that we run cattle for out in Northwest Texas, so when he heard the news about Jack, he took it upon himself to call the man in Northwest Texas and tell him that Jack had left the country and wasn't coming back, which happened to be completely untrue.

James also went down to a piece of property that we lease and told our associates there the same thing—that we were leaving, going out of the country, leaving Alabama, and that he was really surprised we were still in business. That kind of talk, even if it's untrue, is definitely bad for business.

Well, Jack's an easy-going person; he likes to let things go. I do too, to a certain extent, but when you threaten me and my lifestyle, my money and my business, and my family, that gets my blood boiling pretty good.

So, I went to the source. I found James inside his feed store with his wife. Very respectfully I walked in there and I said, "James, can you walk outside with me? We need to talk about something."

So we walked outside and I said, "James, what's the deal with you goin' down to Florala and talkin' to Roy, tellin' him that Jack and I are on our way outta here and that with the way we do business, you're surprised we're still in business?"

He just started kind of mumbling.

I said, "Did we do something wrong to you? Have we offended you in any way? Because we sure do buy a lotta feed from you every week, and you've got a lot of our business. These tubs out here, they're all yours. We buy two tons of feed from you every three weeks. What have we done to you?"

"Oh, y'all ain't done nothin' to me."

So I said, "What's the point in you goin' down there talkin' about us? You don't know me very well. And you sure don't know Jack very well. Why are you goin' around talkin' about us? If you've got somethin' to say about me or Jack or this company, you can call one of us." He's friends with the man that owns the cattle, so I added, "If there's somethin' that you needed to see about some cattle down there, if there's somethin' that you need to know about 'em or wanna go down there and look at 'em, you call me. I'm the only head cowboy for this company, and if you wanna go see 'em, I'll be glad to take you down there.

"But from here on out," I continued, "I don't wanna hear anything else about me or Jack come outta your mouth for Faith Cattle Company because we don't run around talkin' about anybody, and I demand the respect that you won't do that to us.

"So, I'm not comin' up here to start any trouble with you," I said, "but I wanted to come and talk to you man-to-man because I know how towns are—little towns—and how gossip gets stirred up, so I'm comin' to the source. Are we good?"

He said, "We're good."

I said, "See you in a couple days to get some more feed."

So I think that people should go and handle their situations and confront people about the stuff that they're going through because if you don't, if you let time go on by, there's no telling what kind of stories someone's going to come up with or who might get involved. That's why I went to the source then. Jack told me not to, but sometimes you have to, sometimes you just do what you think is right, even though your partner might not think it's right. The big boss man didn't think it was right for me to go say it either.

I just went and took it upon myself because he's there, I'm here, and I've helped build this company and there's a lot on the line.

I'm not saying that keeping your mouth shut, walking away, or turning the other cheek is always the answer. But you have to be smart about how you solve disputes in work and relationships, and it's okay to sometimes step out on a limb. If somebody's saying something about you, confront them; go to the source because like I said, it could be turned around. Remember though, you have to do it calmly, directly, eye-to-eye, and without causing any drama.

When I left there that day, that man respected me way more that afternoon after he got done thinking about what I just did than he did before all this ever even happened.

This happened only a few weeks ago, and now when I see him in town, he's as nice as can be to me. He always waves at me and he reaches out and shakes my hand. That's because I demand respect, and when you start demanding respect from people and also give respect, your life will be a whole lot better.

I didn't yell. I wasn't dramatic. I didn't cuss whatsoever, and I didn't one time look away from his eyes. I looked at him the whole time and was just as calm as could be. I wasn't bowed up. I was just standing there calm and collected but firm.

I just knew I had to get that straightened up because that all goes back to being a protector. A man's supposed to be a protector, and I was protecting Faith Cattle Company, Jack's house, and my house. I was protecting what's mine.

So how does this apply to your love life?

Well, if a woman thinks that her man's doing something or there's an issue between them, they have to go straight to the point and get it fixed up right then and there. You talk about it, and you get it over with. It's not always pleasant, but you see if you can fix the problem and put things back together. If you're a woman, look at it this way. A man is like a horse. He can be a good horse or one that's always gonna buck. If it's unfixable and can't be put back together, then, hey, step off that horse, sell that bad one to somebody else, and go get you a good one because it's just as easy to feed a good one as it is a bad one.

Remember that when you're standing there trying to have a discussion with somebody about a problem, or you're having a problem, whoever plays the drama card first loses. Even when you're in the right.

If you lose your lid and you blow a fuse, all this stuff that you went there to talk to him about doesn't matter because now it's out the window. Now you two are mad at each other and just trying to fight each other. The purpose of you going there—the original problem—never gets solved because it's now sitting over here back in the corner and you two are too busy fighting about something else that doesn't even have anything to do with the original issue at hand.

So stay calm, collected, and cool. I don't care how those so-called Real Housewives on TV deal with their stuff. In your life, talk about the issue at hand. Get that situated and everything will just work itself out.

Nothing will get solved if it starts becoming an egotistical competition. I stayed cool, calm, and collected but firm with that feed salesman. I didn't blow a fuse, and because I did, I was able to get more accomplished when I talked to him. But if I would've lost my lid or blown a fuse, I would've wound up looking like a complete idiot.

When you know an argument or heated conversation is coming up in your life, have a real game plan going in. I think that's the key to the deal.

Ahead of time, I was thinking of all the variables of the situation and of the worst possible things that could happen. I had to get my head together and know what I might do to counteract his gestures. If he was going to be a complete jerk to me or if he was going to cuss me out or if he was going to threaten to whoop me,

I wanted to have already thought of all of these things that I was going to do to kill him with my kindness.

That's what I did on the way down there.

I was saying to myself, "Bubba, you walk in this place and James grabs up a short stick and goes to tryin' to hit you, what're you gonna do? Gonna stand there and defend yourself and say, 'Hey, you know what? This is how you wanna handle your business and this is how you wanna treat people? Then I don't wanna have nothin' to do with you.'"

I have learned in my life that this situation rings true for personal relationships as well as business relationships. If you go to confront your significant other to talk to them about a major issue, I think it's a good idea to have worked through all of the possibilities in your head—good and bad—and to have a game plan. That way, if or when those worst-case scenarios happen, you're prepared and you have an idea of how to act. The person who's the loudest and most dramatic always loses the argument. Cowboys don't get involved in that kind of thing.

The person who stays calm and cool wins.

Every single time.

Eyes

Your words are not as important as your eyes, and never ever will be.

Don't write/text/im/imessage/facetime/skype it – say it.

This is not going to make me very popular with some of the other guys but I am going to say it anyway.

Women, you have a lot of secret weapons. But none of them are as powerful as your eyes.

This is the most important thing you can keep in mind when you have something to say to a man. You have a thought or emotion you need to share – but for some reason you get the overwhelming temptation to sit down at a keyboard and express it to him in five-thousand words and paragraphs and adjectives and superlatives –*right now at this very second.*

This makes no sense. Never before has a man's heart been captured by a great email.

You have emotions and things to say. We want to hear them. But we don't want to read them.

When we read something, we don't hear your voice.

Whether you want to make up or break up, whether you want to change some plans, or tell us something we can do to make you happier than what we are doing, your eyes will never fail you. When we are looking into them, it is the only time we are really hearing you.

If you have something important to say to a guy and you have sent him an email about it – you are making a mistake if you think you have "said what needs to be said".

When you have a thought at 2 O'clock in the morning, and feel like you have to get something off your chest – go ahead and write that long-winded email - if it makes you feel better – and then send it TO YOURSELF – not to him.

Sometimes you want to sit down and write to him, because it makes you feel closer to him. You have something sweet to say. We appreciate these notes, but we love when we can hear the words while your eyes are lighting up right in front of ours.

There is something about emails and texts that makes the communication more instant, but yet way too distant at the same time. Which is not to say we don't like a little flirting and a smile back and forth over text now and then.

But when it comes to anything important, where you want to be really heard, accept no substitute and call in your most powerful weapons.

Just wait until your eyes can deliver the message.

10

A Horse That Bucks
Is Always Gonna Buck

One more word about drama: If you enjoy it, do yourself a favor and go sign yourself up for the next reality show that comes to town. Lock yourself in a house with a bunch of people and lights and cameras because that's where drama comes in wave after wave. One moment everything's fine, we guys would be sitting around on the beach, getting a little sun on our faces, and then the next moment, like a stampede of cattle across the pasture, somebody would come with some issue and start raising their voices and name-calling and hissing and throwing a fit. And I'm talking about a bunch of grown men here! It got ridiculous.

But by now the herd had thinned, so to speak. There were four of us left. We had been through a bunch of activities—overnights in the woods; sniper-rifle shooting out on the range; go-karting; paintball shooting; riding on speedboats, rowboats, and combines; hayrides; archery; and trips to cotton fields, skating rinks, mansions, and karaoke bars. We'd downed an uncountable number of beers and a generous amount of Crown along the way.

They told us going into the deal that this was as close to a fraternity or summer camp as you can get as an adult. And even though there would be times when we would be on each other's nerves, competing for the same beautiful woman, we would be forming a bond and making memories that would last a lifetime.

They were right.

It brought out a lot of emotions in a lot of guys, all that time in the house. A good many of them left there with tears in their eyes, having been told by Paige that she saw them more as friends than anything else.

One of the guys had gotten down on one knee and proposed by a lake, right in the middle of the competition, with a handful of us left in the house. Of course he was crushed when Paige told him she cared for him but not in the way a wife needs to care for a husband. He got the ring back and left crushed. That guy was not exactly a favorite among all of us in that house, and that's no secret if you watch the show.

Yeah, we all took a little bit of pleasure in hearing how he had bent down and asked for her hand, only to be handed the ring back and sent packing and out the gate. I could feel myself delighted with it all as it went down. I regret that. Part of the Cowboy Code is never kicking a man when he's down.

No matter what he's done to you, or what your feelings are about his character, when a man's hurting, the right thing to do is to be on that high road and help him out. A real cowboy will do that. No matter what's happened in the past, we stop and help the other guy change a tire when he's got a flat. We'll help him harvest a field when he's under the gun to get the job done.

Now, I'm not saying I don't hold grudges because I do. And I wish I could say I've always walked a straight line and taken that high road and never wished ill onto others, but I haven't. There've been lots of times when I've been very angry, or let down, or mad, and could feel myself really cursing someone and hoping that karma would come around and take its revenge.

But that's all energy wasted. So when we watched that poor guy drag his luggage off the front porch, all dejected and lovesick, and when he walked off from under the lights and we all started laughing and enjoying the moment, I felt bad. That was wrong.

I tried to say to the other guys, "Hey, look, let's not kick the ol' boy when he just got punched in the gut."

Everyone kind of laid off him after that.

So the next time you feel yourself taking pleasure in someone else's misery or downfall, try reaching out a hand instead. It'll make you a better person.

These elimination nights would roll around and there was a very animalistic element to them. It would start in the afternoons as everyone would be told to pack up all their things in the suitcases just in case you were the one to get the ol' boot out the door. Everyone would get very serious and quiet. There's something very primal about being in a group and not wanting to be singled out as the weak one in the herd.

I've been around big, proud, strong animals my whole life and I've learned a bunch of things from them.

The trick to raising cattle is to work as hard as you possibly can to make sure those cows never feel stress. Stress is the enemy. When a cow's under stress, that's when they get all crazy in the mind. They start stewing around, they stop eating, and they start backing up on you (losing weight).

The cowboy game is getting those cattle properly conditioned, fat, growing, and healthy. Keep the stress off 'em. Grass turns to fat, fat turns to beef, and beef turns to money. Once stress enters the picture, it all starts going downhill.

It was the same thing with us humans in the house. Once the stress of elimination hit, everyone's weaknesses and vulnerabilities started coming out. Guys were lookin' over their shoulders, worried, jittery. It made them nervous around Paige, and if there is one thing women don't like, it's a guy who's giving off a vibe of insecurity.

When we raise cattle we get up real early and saddle up and head out to the pasture at first light. Like I said, we work from "can to can't"—from when you can see the sun as it just comes up to when it dips below the horizon.

Personally, I love to sleep and nothing makes me happier than a long, lazy morning, but no matter what kind of nonsense has gone on the night before, we get up and out as early as we do for good reason. Because when you get out and look at the cattle in the early morning, that's when you can tell which of them are walking tall and which are falling off and need doctoring.

It's just like a little kid—first thing in the morning is when you can tell if they're sniffling, or slower than usual, or carrying a fever. By the middle of the day, all kids kind of make their way around the playground, and you can't pick them out as well. But first thing in the morning is when they'll tell you that they're under the weather.

Well, it's the same thing with cattle. They're like little kids, only they weigh about 200 to 800 pounds and when they get sick, things can go south in a real hurry. I've seen one of them get something and give it to the rest of them, and before you know it, a whole herd gets thinned out and drops out on you almost overnight. So we're out there at daybreak so we can tend to the weaker calves right away. We rope them off and give them a shot of vitamins and hope that does the trick.

You can just tell by the way a cow holds its head, or curls in its shoulders, or slouches its back that it's losing confidence. It's gonna be a step slower today and that means it's gonna be two steps slower tomorrow and maybe dead by the day after.

Well, I could see the same thing happening in that house full of guys, especially on those elimination nights. You could see their shoulders start falling off, their heads getting lower, their eyes darting around the room.

I never went there. In my mind, I stayed full of confidence. That's not being cocky, or at least I hope it isn't coming off that way. Trust me, I have as many insecurities as the next guy, and I'm not ashamed to admit it. I've already told you (and Paige) how nervous I was feeling and those butterflies I was getting. But when it came to those big moments, when some were gonna be chosen to stay and others were gonna be sent away, I wasn't nervous then. I kept my shoulders back.

First, Paige would come up the back porch and have a cold beer with us. She'd usually say something nice to all of us to tell us how wonderful we were making her feel, and we'd all be listening for one word ....

"But ...," she would say as the sentence hinged like a wrought-iron gate, "tonight I have to say goodbye to three more of you."

I made sure that during these little speeches my shoulders were always back, my head up, and when Paige's eyes would lock on mine, I always had a sense that I wasn't going anywhere. I believe if you carry yourself that way, you can affect the outcome in life.

Then Boyd would come next, kind of like the Grim Reaper of Love, trudging up the stairway. His eyes ran over the bunch of us like a Powercraft 4M Candle Power Rechargeable Halogen Spotlight shining out the window of a slowly moving 4-by-4 looking for rabbits or raccoons to shoot up.

Guys would just freeze.

I've seen a lot of deer caught in the headlights like that in my life, but I'd never seen it literally happen to grown men before. Boyd wouldn't try that stuff on me though.

These elimination nights were hard on me because I knew I'd be saying good-bye to more roommates I had grown fond of. But I was never going into those nights thinking there was even a chance I was on the way out the gate. There's one more area where I think there's a good parallel between men and livestock, and I think it can be helpful to some women to think of it this way.

It centers on a phrase us cowboys like to use: "A horse that bucks is always gonna buck."

Some men, like horses, can be trained. We train 1,200-pound horses to do what we want them to do, and hopefully, some of those lessons also apply to how to get a guy to do some of the little things you want him to do to make you happy and feel more appreciated.

I buy colts and train them and turn them into horses. They're used for tools. I know a lot of people have them for pets, and that's all good, but cowboys believe a horse is happiest when he has a job to do and is being used as a tool.

A colt is a young horse between the ages of three and five. You've got a little old stud colt, which is a male, or a filly, which is a female.

Technically I'm not what you would call a horse whisperer. I know a few, and they are the elite men and women who can do pretty much anything with a wild one and make it tame. I don't use the "whisperer" word too often; it's more of a myth than a fact. More common is a cowboy or cowgirl who is just a "hand." In many ways that's one of the highest compliments we have around my place, to call someone a "hand" is to say he or she is good—a teacher. Hands have the determination to get this horse's respect and that's pretty much what it is.

You can't do much with a colt. You sure enough can't get on his back until he's two because his back's not fully developed until he's two years old. A horse will never become a horse until he has a job.

A lot of times people will have a horse that they rode for 30 to 60 days and say he's broke. But he's not broke. He's not broke until he's had a job for a few years.

The first step that I always try to do is to build a bond, a relationship with that horse. When you first put a colt that's never been touched or handled off in a round pen, he's going to do everything he can to get away from you. As he's in the pen, I'll try and make slow movements with my shoulders tilted down because if you walk around with your shoulders built up, he's thinking you're fixing to come at him and hurt him.

So I go in there, relaxed, with my shoulders down. I always take a few steps toward the colt and as he's getting away from me, I try to back up away from him as soon as I can. And he notices. "Hey, he's kind of coming at me a couple steps and then he's backing off. He's kind of relieving the pressure."

Horses work off of pressure. Man is kind of the same way.

If a girl's coming at you really hard and strong, like they've done me in the past, I'm backing up. I'm full-force getting back from them because I want to be comfortable when somebody's coming toward me—same thing goes for a colt.

Just a few days ago I was messing with a new one, and I walked up to her, and she just took off running from me to the pen. She ran right into the pen. So, I stopped for a few minutes and relaxed and waited for her to calm down. Then I tilted my shoulders down, walked toward her a little bit, and then I stopped and backed up away from her.

So, I put on a little pressure and then I backed off; I relieved the pressure. And before you know it, I could walk right up to her and almost touch her. She'd get nervous and start shaking, and I'd stop and back up, and then I could hear her breathing.

Relax.

As the day went on, I was rubbing her all over, loving on her, and I could walk up to her and back up and then all of a sudden, she'd come toward me and want to be scratched. So, it's kind of like building a relationship. Those are the first few days of training, and they're important. Before you ever just throw a saddle on her, you have to spend that time with her because if you just grab a hold of one, you make her nervous. Put a saddle on a nervous horse and climb up on her, she's going to do everything she can to get out from underneath you.

The same thing happens in relationships: If one of you is being real pushy or trying to be real forward and coming on real strong, the other's gonna go the other way.

Another thing that we do whenever we have a colt is we try to get that respect, to let them know that we're not going to hurt him. He has to learn to work off of your body movement. He has to earn a bond and trust you that you're not going to put him in harm's way. You may get him right there next to it, but he's got to learn that you're not going to get him hurt. That's when the horse really starts becoming a horse, when they start knowing, "Hey, this guy's just run me clear across this field, jumped me over 14 creeks, and come to a complete halt." They trust you to lead them into anything.

What does this teach you about trust? It's an amazing feeling to have one that you can trust because there are so many of them out there that you can't trust—so many that buck you off and hurt you. Well, once you get hurt, a lot of that trust is gone. It's the same with a relationship. If you're dating somebody and he tells you he's going out with his buddies tonight and then your girlfriend sees him out at the bar with another girl, you're hurt and a lot of your trust is gone.

That horse is always gonna buck.

We need our horses to be okay running right up to 1200-pound cattle. Some horses hate circling those cows (we call those "cowey" horses), but we need to put our lives in the hands of horses who can keep their cool surrounded by giant cattle. On a moment's notice they need to sprint behind a loose cow, in a full-on dead run pull in behind the cow, wait for us to throw a rope, and then stop on a dime and take the weight of that rope choking off a thousand pounds of running beef.

Horses don't naturally love this, but we're counting on them and they're counting on us. We're partners out there in that pasture together. It's a relationship we're in together out there, and both of our lives and livelihoods depend on the other.

We work those horses really hard when they are acting up. But the important part of the equation is when they are doing the job correctly we reward them. Big time.

Say for instance, I've been training one of my colts to rope calves. I want him to go from 0 to 40 miles an hour and stop on a dime—just stop like that. The first four or five times he may not go. He may run his heart out and get that calf and then kind of dribble to a stop.

Well, he didn't do what I wanted to do.

So, we're going to do it again—just repetition, muscle memory. And as soon as he leaves that box, tracks that cow, and stops on a dime just like I wanted him to, I step off him and unsaddle him right there. He takes a deep breath and relaxes. And then tomorrow, he remembers, "Hey, I had to run five or six times to get this calf, but the time I ran as hard as I could and I stopped, my job was done."

So, it's kind of like a woman getting her man to do things. She may have to get him to do it four or five times and he may hate it, but when he does what she wants him to do, everything's good to go—just step off and reward him.

Men are lazy. We love to be rewarded and we love to work less, not more. When we get something right, reward us. Don't forget to do that. It is the single-best way of getting what you want from an untrained colt, and to some extent the same methods will work on your man.

One of my horses—a horse that's usually a great one—wants to buck me off once in a while. Or he'll want to try me and give me attitude. He wants to kick up. He wants to swish his tail around and throw his head in the air. He loves to act up every once in a while even though he knows better than that.

When that happens, when he's been broke and trained but he's giving me a problem, I need to work him all day long. Sometimes, I tie him up to the back of the trailer and drive him five miles from the ranch back to the house and he's running his ass off the whole way home.

That's called, "If you're not going to listen to me, I'm going to make you listen and you're either going to make it or you're out of here."

It's just as easy to feed a good horse as it is a bad one, which is true for relationships too. It's just as easy to put in all this time and effort into building a good relationship as it is a bad one, so why not put it into a good relationship?

If you see things in your relationship that aren't making you happy and you're saying to yourself, "I don't know if this is gonna work, and I don't like this about him"—just stop. Get out of it. Get off that horse and get you another one because there are so many of them out there it's just as easy to have a good one as it is to have a bad one. After all, there are some men who cannot be trained.

I had that talk with a girl not too long ago about a guy treating her bad, always accusing her of running around. I said, "He's accusin' you of runnin' around because he's runnin' around on you. He doesn't want you to have any guy friends because he's got tons of girlfriends, and that's just how it is."

Regarding men who abuse women and would raise a hand to them, I have zero respect for them. I think they should be taken out back and beaten with a wooden stick then nailed to a stump as you light the stump on fire.

Men that prey on women and beat on women, I think they're absolutely worthless. God made us men to protect women, not to beat them down. He gave us strength and wisdom and we're put on this Earth to protect them, not harm them. I have no tolerance for mentally and physically abusing a woman, no real cowboy does.

Like we always say, "If he's a whoopin' up on you now and y'all are just now dating, y'all ain't even married, what's he gonna do when y'all get married and have children and the children are pissin' him off and he's got done whoopin' them? When he comes inside after spankin' 'em outside with a switch, and you didn't wash his pants for tomorrow, what's he gonna do? Is he gonna beat you down too?"

A situation like that is only going to get worse. Things like that don't get better. Again, what we always say is, "A horse that bucks is always gonna buck."

That sums it up: A horse that bucks is always gonna buck. He may ride good for two days, but you know any minute he could blow up and put you on your head and break your neck. I'm a firm believer in that because it's happened. I've unfortunately seen it too many times.

Sometimes I see women in this situation and half of the time they don't want to leave their relationship that they're in because they're afraid. The problem is that he's beat them up too bad already, battered them up and beaten their emotions down so badly that they're afraid to leave.

But that's such nonsense.

I have a dear friend who's in one of these relationships. Truthfully none of us know the real story behind it, but we all have our suspicions. This is a girl who projects the air of confidence from a mile away. She's gorgeous, smart, and funny. She's the last person in the world you would ever expect to be putting up with a scumbag of a guy. But that's what's going on behind the scenes.

They'll argue and he'll call her a "whore" or tell her she's nothing but "scum" and "trash." And the next day she'll go crawling back to him.

As her friends, we've all been trying to break the pattern, but it's difficult, and it's been going on like this for years. In the back of her mind is the notion that "maybe he'll change." But, like a horse that's prone to buck, guys like this don't change.

Ladies, you don't deserve this for a single second of this life.

I've had this conversation with my friend, and it goes something like this:

"Okay, look. You don't deserve to be treated like that. You need to get all your stuff together and get out of that relationship because it's not gonna get any better. You've been doing this for how many months now? It's just not gonna get any better. Every time you think it's getting good, something happens and it gets worse. It really does get worse. There's no fixin' it.

"There's just no sense in you putting up with it. You've got too much to offer. You don't deserve it. You're too beautiful of a person and your morals are great. There's somebody out there that will respect you for the way you are and for what you are, and you just need to get your stuff together and get going."

When I had this conversation with her, I remember her telling me she was just so scared. She didn't want to start dating somebody else because she was afraid he was going to show up and try to whoop them and all this other stuff. He'd hurt her trust and that's something that she can't ever get back.

That's the same way with us cowboys. If we got a horse that we don't trust half the time, chances are we're not even gonna fool with him. And if we are gonna fool with him, we're gonna work him to the bone before he earns an ounce of trust again. In the front of our mind we're thinking, "He's tried to hurt us."

So, to cut all that nonsense out, if you have something that you don't trust, get rid of it. A horse that bucks when he's young is always gonna buck.

A man that cheats, or lies, or steals, or hurts you is always going to do that. There's no way around it.

He may be good for five years, but in that moment you let him go, let the reins loose so he can just start rolling out in that pasture, he'll buck you again. He hasn't done it in five years, but he did it a long time ago when he was young. He's going to do it again.

That's a lesson many a cowboy has learned the hard way.

Relationships? It's the same thing.

11

KNOWING WHEN IT'S WORTH IT

There were now four of us left in the house, and today it was gonna go from four to two. After three weeks of laying my heart out there, feeling things that I hadn't felt in years, it was another of those times to reach inside and search for the words and the emotions I was feeling and find a way to let them all out.

I wasn't worried in the least. I was riding a wave of feeling up there in the clouds, full of positive thoughts about falling in love and living happily ever after, as old fashioned as that sounds. But I had no idea what I was going to say in this last little private time we each had with Paige before she made this next cut.

I decided I wasn't going to plan it out. I was just going to live in the moment and enjoy the quiet time together, letting whatever happened happen. To be honest, I was tired of thinking about this as an "audition," and it felt like we were equal in our feelings for each other. I had it in my mind that a higher plan had brought us together, and that as crazy as this whole outing had been, it was part of some other plan to bring two people together who were going to be very deeply in love.

However, Jeremiah, the farmer from Minnesota who had been in that scuffle a week or so ago, was a wreck about the whole deal. He didn't know what he was feeling, and the thought of sharing it was even worse. He was wired differently than the rest of us.

I felt like I really knew all the guys in that house well, but none of us really knew him. We didn't know what made him tick, or what his values were. He was distant and aloof. For a while we all thought he was just chill and laid back. But when you live with someone under the same roof for the better part of a month and you still don't feel like you know them all that well, something's a little off.

We all drove over to the Oak Hollow Ranch where Paige was waiting on us. In the van it was real quiet, and the guy talk had kind of subsided. It was in moments like this where all of our friendships with each other dropped off and we realized we were all different competitors chasing after the same dream.

But Jeremiah was spooked like a horse that had been saddled for the first time. His eyes were darting around. He was all fidgety. He wore a bandana on his head all the time. Maybe that bandana was on there too tight—I don't know—but the guy was so nervous he was spooking the rest of us a little bit.

The night before, Paige sent in two of her girlfriends to take all of us guys out, and, I suppose, get a sense for our intentions. I wasn't worried about it. A girl's friends usually like me, and I had a great time getting to know Paige's friends. They told me her nickname is "Paigekins," and I could see "Bubba and Paigekins" going together real well.

Jeremiah had a little too much to drink around her friends and apparently didn't pay too much attention to them. His attitude was he didn't need to impress anyone. He even spilled a drink of whiskey on one of their shoes.

He broke off from the group and got up on stage at the honky-tonk bar to play some of his music. He was in a band and half the time was hoping this television experience would help him sell music. Let's just say the performance up there on stage was a little sloppy: All the amps came unplugged, and it was kind of a disaster. It was no way to win favor with a girl's friends.

After hearing about that, and knowing that he froze up when Paige expressed her feelings for him, I didn't see Jeremiah as much of a threat. A guy who can't process how he's feeling isn't in the right place to treat a woman like Paige the way she deserves to be treated.

Jeremiah met up with Paige first, though, and went out into the field while the rest of us guys waited around at the barn for about a half hour before he returned. He looked worse coming back than he did going out there. He was crying—not teary, I mean really breaking down, pacing around, holding his head in his hands. He asked the crew members to take him back to the house right away so he could be alone. He was headed for another day in bed, curled up, and freaked out.

Yeah, that was one guy who didn't stand much of a chance in the end in my eyes.

A bigger threat loomed in my eyes from the most unlikely source of all—my friend from New York City, Shaun Bigos. Ol' Bigos had returned from a date a little while back chasing gators through a Louisiana swamp all smitten. The kid was still wearing a navy blazer and still heading to the tanning booth almost every day, but after a few dates with Paige and a few weeks in the Southern air, he was singing a very different tune.

His new favorite phrase was, "I have embraced the South." And the truth was we'd embraced him as well.

I could see Paige was attracted to him. He made her blush a little bit. There was something about the lure of that lifestyle that a lot of women from around here find fascinating. A lot of them wonder "Can I make it up there?" and even more have that saying in their minds, "I've got to make it out of this town." I didn't think Paige was like that though. In my heart I always felt she was a country girl, and she knew her place was down here.

There was a territorial aspect to the fight for her heart—us versus them—and that added to the desire to "get" her or "win" her. But the truth of the matter was I wasn't trying to win over Paige to represent the South; I wanted her for myself, and for the way she was making me feel.

I had every curve of her body memorized. She would walk by and just the way her legs moved and her hair slid from side to side would get my mind wandering. It made me think about sitting next to her, taking long plane rides together, or maybe just resting in rocking chairs, facing west at the end of the day.

It made me think about being the young couple that kissed a little too much in public. It made me think about being the old couple in church on Sundays that still held hands after all those years.

She was on my mind from the moment I woke up in the morning to the moment I went to sleep at night. As the song says, "I want to know how forever feels." This was as close as I'd ever come.

If there was one guy left in the mix that could take that away from me now it was Shaun from New York. I wasn't just up against him; I was up against everything he might represent to a young woman who could light up any town, from the smallest one-stop-sign dive in the South to the biggest, brightest city in the world.

I knew Shaun was feeling a lot of the same things I was feeling. And I knew he was man enough to seize this kind of moment and lay his feelings out there. As he walked out to the meadow to meet up with Paige, I got a little quiet.

He came back confident, head high. He has a lot of honesty, and he told her she had changed his views about a lot of things, and he liked that. Another thing Paige did was challenge him, and confront him, and push back from time to time. He was big enough to recognize he needed some of that in his life as well. The phrase he used was, "She can put me in my place."

He wasn't ready to pick up and move all the way down here, but he was willing to meet her half way, and there was something practical about that for Paige as well. During her time in NASCAR, she had seen all the big cities. But maybe there was some middle ground where the two of them could live and start a life.

Well there wasn't much I could do about that but be happy for the guy.

And get ready.

Yeah, Shaun was the one to beat: a guy with a $400-a-month hairspray habit versus a dirty, lifelong cowboy from the Deep South.

Damn crazy if you ask me.

I got out there and met Paige in the middle of one of Boyd's greenest pastures. It was perfect. There were quarter horses running all around. As we sat under a giant oak tree, the horses kind of closed in on us and walked all around.

> PAIGE: (To Camera) I can't think of a better place to sit and talk with Bubba than in two homemade wooden chairs surrounded by this beautiful herd of horses. My heart's so happy just sittin' there waitin' for him.
>
> PAIGE: Hey, cowboy.
>
> BUBBA: Hey, cowgirl. How are you?

PAIGE: Good, how are you?

BUBBA: Good to see you.

PAIGE: Good to see you too. My friends had fun with you last night.

BUBBA: They're awesome. They're lovely ladies, they are.

PAIGE: Yeah, they're like, "Oh, we love Bubba." They, like, talked about nicknames, everything.

BUBBA: Yeah, Paigekins. I told them that, you know, I'm really glad that I'm here and got to meet you, you know?

PAIGE: Me too.

BUBBA: I mean really, from the bottom of my heart, Paige.

PAIGE: Me too.

PAIGE: (To Camera) Everything about Bubba is perfect, and I just need to figure out what's goin' through Bubba's mind because he's the guy I've dreamed about spending the rest of my life with.

PAIGE: How are you feelin'?

BUBBA: I feel good. I feel good. I, uh, really have major feelin's for you, Paige. And, uh, I have a hard time sleepin' at nighttime.

PAIGE: Why?

BUBBA: 'Cause I'm thinkin' about you, you know? And, uh, it's hard for me to talk about my feelin's just 'cause I'm ... that ... that's how I am but, uh, you definitely bring that out in me and, you know, I wanna give you all my feelin's, my whole heart. I really do ... so ...

BUBBA: (To Camera) I've waited my whole life where I could meet a woman like Paige. I mean, I'm just so excited.

BUBBA: (To Camera) I'm blushin' right now. I'm nervous. My knees are a little weak, you know? She makes me smile all the time. I can't quit thinkin' about her. She has definitely stolen my heart.

PAIGE: You're everything, everything I've always wanted, and you're everything I wanna be. Like I wanna be the person you are. You just have it all together, and you have your life together, and you take care of things, you do.

BUBBA: Almost, but the only thing that's missin' is you.

PAIGE: You would be the person I would want to raise my kids and everything's just, you're exactly what every girl would want.

BUBBA: I've never met anybody as nice and sweet and just genuine as you are, you know? I mean, you're a strong woman. I've always prayed for a strong woman. People, you know, always say, "When you know, you know," and, uh, and I know that it's right.

PAIGE: This is so pretty.

BUBBA: You know, I mean this, this right here, what you see, this is the lifestyle that you'll have with me. You know— horses and the cattle and of course goin' out and havin' a good time and hanging out with friends. Just a good Southern life, you know? And I'll cook for you all the time. We may have to watch what we eat though.

[LAUGHTER]

PAIGE: Please, I gotta figure to keep up.

[LAUGHTER]

PAIGE: I know. This is where I'm happiest. This is so beautiful to me and I, it just makes me happy, this.

BUBBA: Well you make me happy.

PAIGE: You make me happy too.

BUBBA: And, uh, I just thank the Lord every night, you know, that He's put you in my life.

PAIGE: Me too.

BUBBA: And, and I don't want you to go anywhere.

PAIGE: I know.

BUBBA: Except back home with me.

PAIGE: [LAUGHS] With all my cowboy boots, in your closet.

BUBBA: Yeah, yeah, we're gonna have to expand the closet a little bit. I'll just give you my closet, how about that?

PAIGE: Okay, I want the big one.

BUBBA: That's fine, that's fine. I'll move my stuff upstairs. I really do care about you. And, uh, it is tough, sittin' around the house and hearin' somebody else, you know, say that they really care about you and I'm thinkin', 'Well, he better care about her a whole lot 'cause I care about her,' you know?

PAIGE: Oh, Bubba. Well, I care about you too, and I just, you make me a better person.

BUBBA: You make me a better person.

PAIGE: You make me a better person. You can't get any better.

PAIGE: (To Camera) This is the guy I've always looked for. It's so serious with him. He's not playin' any games. He's such a man, and he can just look you in the eyes and you know he's tellin' you the truth.

BUBBA: Well, I wanna tell you that I'm fallin' in love with you.

PAIGE: You do?

BUBBA: Yeah, I am. And, um, I would be devastated if you went off with somebody else. And I don't want that to happen.

PAIGE: I don't want to either.

BUBBA: I don't want that to happen at all. I want this lifestyle for me and you.

[HORSE SNORTS BY PAIGE'S HEAD]

PAIGE: He says yes.

BUBBA: You like that too, don't you Baldy, huh? You like that too, don't ya? Huh?

PAIGE: Ah, thank you for tellin' me that. I fall more in love with you every time I see you. Like every time I see you, I'm just like, ah, this is the most amazing person I've ever met.

BUBBA:	Well, I know when you and me look in each other in the eyes, it's real. It's not just, you know, stupid stuff. This is real. This is real. I've always wanted nothin' but the best, and now that I got it, you know, I'm excited.
PAIGE:	Thanks, Bubba.
BUBBA:	And I want you, forever.
	[BUBBA AND PAIGE KISS]

There was a word there that I had never used with a woman before.

Forever.

I hadn't planned it and I hadn't thought about it. I just felt it. I felt the Lord had blessed me. I had prayed for a feeling like this for such a long time and here it was, coming true, in the perfect place in the shade of an oak tree.

	[HORSE SNORTS – PAIGE AND BUBBA LAUGH]
PAIGE:	Let's just hop on 'em and go ride off. Let's go ride off in the sunset, again.
BUBBA:	You want to? We'll have many times to do that. I promise you.
	[BUBBA AND PAIGE KISS]

That night Paige had her decisions to make. She sat outside on the back of her pickup truck, lights twinkling in the trees above her, and let us know who the final two were going to be.

Cowboy Shaun Smith went home first. He was torn up about it, but he was still in college, and I think we all knew he and Paige were not in the same place in their lives.

The next to go home was Shaun Bigos. He was headed back to New York. As crude as he was on the way in, that's how much class he had on the way out. He looked me in the eye and shook my hand like a cowboy. I knew I'd made a friend for life. I was sorry to see him go, but I was sure that with just myself and Jeremiah left, I was surely on my way to ending up with Paige in the end.

What was our life going to be like together?

I knew exactly.

Because for all the rough rides my mom and my sisters had been through when it came to relationships and men—and in my mom's case, a very sad divorce—I'm blessed in my life with the perfect role models of a long-lasting love and marriage—my grandparents.

My grandfather's name is Floyd Thompson, and he's always been the man that I've turned to for advice and guidance. My grandmother, Irma Lee, she crafted me. She was always a classy lady, always dressed to a T, but she was also a hard worker. And she always demanded to be treated like a lady from my grandfather, which is the only way he does things anyway.

I'd always watch how she held herself and how my grandfather treated her and what she demanded, and also how she treated him and always served him. They just always worked together as a couple. Watching their relationship has helped craft me.

She kind of taught me how to be a gentleman too. She'd always say, "Now, Bubba, you get out and open this door for your aunt that's gettin' out of that car," and things like that. She'd guide me along on what I needed to do, and I remember one time, she about snatched my hair off my head because I was walking down the street with her and she said, "You get on this side of the road."

She said, "You're a man here and you're supposed to protect us from oncoming traffic or whatever may come our way, so you're standing on this side of the street."

I was downtown with her and we were walking to the drug store. They served homemade vanilla Coke and grape soda and things like that, and we were walking from Pounds Motor Company, which was a tractor place. (The man that owns Pounds Motor Company was actually the man that invented the first rubber tractor tire; I got to meet him as a kid.)

Anyway, we were headed to the drugstore to get a vanilla Coke, and I was walking, just hopping along, and she grabbed me by my flat-top blonde hair and said, "You get on over here, grandson. This is where you walk as a young man—whenever you're courting a lady."

She said, "This is how you do it, and you always open the doors, and say 'yes, sir—no, sir.' You even say, 'yes, sir—no, sir,' or 'yes ma'am—no ma'am' to your woman that you're courting."

Trust me, I remember to do all of that to this day. I'll always remember that she taught me to protect women from danger, whatever it may be. I was probably about seven or eight years old.

Now they're both 88. My grandfather grew up in Georgia as a little boy and then they moved to Florida. He's from a family of, I believe, 14 brothers and sisters, and he's a big-time athlete, ball player, and he wound up dating a cheerleader—my grandmother—from the rival town.

They ended up getting married and he had a furniture business, and then they also had the nursery business—that was their main thing. After that, my whole family worked in the nursery business and grew plants.

He's a classy guy—a straight-up classy gentleman. He'll work hard all day long, and then if he's got to run to town to pick up something or go to the store for a Coke, he goes home and changes so that he does not go into town looking dirty, no matter what. He's always been like that—always in tip-top shape and always looks good wherever he goes. He's got a lot of wisdom, and he's been able to see a world go from no telephones to computers. He's seen it all, every bit of it.

My grandfather is my number one role model. I've always looked up to him because he's always succeeded in everything that he's ever done or everything that he's touched has just turned to gold. I've always wanted to follow in his footsteps, and he's always taught me how to treat people with respect even if they don't treat you nice—just kill 'em with kindness. That's the way I've always done, and I think that's the reason I am the way that I am because I've spent so much time listening to my grandfather and learning from him. We all lived on the same piece of property and I would ride either the three-wheeler or the golf cart up to his place and spend time with him.

Every spring we always put a garden together. We would always disc up in between the orange trees right there behind the back of his house and plant a garden—corn and okra—and we'd just sit there and talk. He'd sit there and peel oranges for me with his old-timer knife, and I'd be eating them as fast as he could peel them.

Wherever he'd go, he'd always take me with him, take me to get my hair cut or go eat breakfast with him and all of his buddies when I was a little kid. We kept all of our horses at his place too, so I would go up there and saddle up my little pony and just ride around and he'd ride around with me.

Whenever I was having a rough time with something or, in between high school or hunting for a job and money was hard to come by, he'd always tell me, "It's always darkest just before dawn." That was a big saying with my grandfather. He's said it to me on many occasions. And he's always been right.

And another of his favorite sayings was explaining how he's stayed married to my grandmother for 60-plus years. His secret?

He told me that he was the head of the house and he always had the last two words in any argument: "Yes, ma'am."

He said that's the answer to a good marriage: Always get your last two words in and they better be, "Yes, ma'am," and when she said, "Jump," he always said, "How high?"

I think he always said that "Yes ma'am" to her because if they were arguing or mad at each other, whenever it came down to the end of the conversation, if she was upset and he was upset, he'd rather say, "Yes, ma'am," and agree with her and keep her happy. He's a man and he's gonna get over it eventually and he can just go on about his life. So in order to make his day go by better and keep the relationship good, it was just always the respectful thing to say, "Yes, ma'am," or "Okay, honey. I understand," or "That'll be fine. We'll just do that." He could just take it on the chin and go on.

I think that's part of being a man too.

Sometimes you just have to let your pride go. Pride gets in the way of a lot of people's relationships all the time, like with two hardheaded people. It's a pride issue. It says in the Bible, "Pride comes before a fall," and if you're real prideful, bad things are gonna happen.

You think: You're a man, and in your mind you're programmed to believe you're supposed to be the head honcho. You're supposed to comfort your loved ones, be strong for them, and be that shield for them.

That's all part of it. But in the same sentence, you also have to be a sensitive type of person. You have to understand at the end of the argument, if the argument ever even stops, and you say, "Okay, baby," or "Yes, ma'am," or "Okay, we'll do this," or if you agree with her and compromise with her, that lets her know that you didn't necessarily give in to her, but that you love her enough to make room for her feelings.

It doesn't always feel great in the moment, but in a higher way it is the right thing to do a lot of the times.

When it comes to the ideal marriage, my grandparents' relationship is what I compare things to. They always talk things over, and they always have to compromise and agree on things. It's never one-sided. In many ways, I'm looking for somebody that's going to love me like my grandmother loves my grandfather. She'd always stood by his side, always, and still does to this day and that's what I'm after.

I think that's what everybody else should be after—finding that one person that makes them realize they can't see themselves with anybody else.

I always go to my grandfather for advice whenever I'm having trouble with something or with the cattle or business. He'll just tell me to pull my hat down and go through it, and to pray about it and things will always work out the way they're supposed to. He's 88 years old, and he always comes to me and tells me, "Hey, you need to go talk to this person," or "You need to figure out what's going on and I need you to fix it."

I'm the only boy to carry on my last name. I'm the only Thompson left out of our whole entire family to carry on our name, and he just looks at me as if I'm like the little prince of the family who will be the one running the show one day.

With a grandfather that's such a good guy and a gentleman and that has always treated people nice and tends to business, I can't imagine my goal being anything other than to live like him.

But it's different if you've got a role model that's a guy that stays out and parties all night long or is running around on his wife and things like that. The saying is the apple doesn't fall far from the tree. So, that's exactly what's going to happen. A guy will often end up being just like his role model, or close to it.

That's why it's important to ask a man about this early on. You'll get an idea of who he is and who he wants to be. It will paint a very good picture of his morals, his goals, and his intentions.

Both my grandfather and my grandmother worked. They worked to have a family and they worked at their relationship, and if they hadn't, they wouldn't have all that they have now. They both pulled their weight and made the relationship work. They've been at it so long that they make it look easy, but spend some time around them and you realize that you have to work to make a relationship work. It's just not going to work on its own.

It's about balance, about saying yes, picking your battles, respecting your partner, and knowing what's worth it. And trying to end your conversations by warmly and fondly saying, "yes ma'am".

Loosen the reigns

There is something about the outside of a horse that is good for the inside of a man. – Winston Churchill

You can tell a lot about someone by the way they sit in the saddle.

I consider myself a pretty good rider. But there are a lot of cowboys out there who are even better.

The thing that's easiest to spot is when someone is just not at home on horseback. These are the guys who are yanking the horses head back and forth, always fighting to stay centered, and pulling on the reigns left and right. They're cursing at their horse, and you can see the horse biting down on the bit in anger. It can't wait to get the bridle off and feel whole again.

That animal needs to be respected. If you know what you're doing, the horse you're on can tell what you want him to do just with the slightest of movement. A little nudge here and there, a slight amount of pressure from your leg. When you're in harmony with that horse it's like the two of you are thinking the same thing at the same time.

When it isn't going so well, he can feel like 1500 pounds of angry animal just waiting for the right moment to bog his head and send you flying.

The same thing goes for relationships. I hear women talking about the tight grip they have on their guy, almost as if that's bragging rights, and I know that never works.

The harder you pull back on those reigns, the more that horse's gums bleed, eventually he is going to buck you off at the worst moment possible.

When we break our new colts we let them know whose boss for sure. If they put us in a dangerous spot or fail to get the job done, we let them know, and hopefully they learn from it.

Men will respond to the same type of nurturing. When the situation calls for it, you let us know, and we will not forget it.

But day in and day out, if you are tight on the reigns, we are going to feel it. And what we, like horses, feel is not strength, but insecurity and doubt.

You have to give us some room to run. If your guy wants to head out to spend a night with the boys and cut loose a little, consider loosening the reigns and letting him do it without any payback, or mean glances, or curt phone calls.

Your girlfriends might object. One of them might even say *"oh I would never let my guy get away with that!"*

But the experienced rider knows to let go and ease up.

The rider who is most comfortable and confident in the saddle is the one who often lets loose on those reigns and controls their horse through constant communication, not pressure to the teeth.

That's how a cowboy stays strong in the saddle.

12

PULLING YOUR HAT DOWN

The way the final stretch of this show was going to work was that we were each going to have one final day and evening with Paige.

One thing I liked was that on this show, unlike some of the others, there were no overnight dates. We had all signed a long contract saying we understood that things stay pretty G-rated in the courtship. I think this was a good thing on many levels—mainly that it allowed you to get to know one another without any of the pressure of getting too physical. It was also very much in line with the values of the South. It wouldn't be right for a young lady to spend a night with one guy one night, and then spend the next night with another guy.

It was bad enough thinking about her being in someone else's arms for an evening—and that was about to happen.

After telling Jeremiah and me what was going to happen over the next couple days, she chose to take Jeremiah out first, leaving me for the very end. Well, as far as I was concerned, that was fitting. I liked the idea of going last and riding off with her into the sunset. But I hated knowing she and Jeremiah would be off somewhere together tomorrow.

It was a northern farmer versus a Southern cowboy.

We'd all shook hands on the deal, but inside I knew there was nothing natural about this. In some ways, I was fine knowing I had a whole house of guys to edge out. But when it got down to just myself and one other guy, it all seemed very real.

The next morning Jeremiah got up early, put on the same bandana he had been wearing for four weeks, and headed out the door. I was alone in that mansion on the water, and the quiet in the house was eerie.

There wasn't a cloud in the sky as the water lapped up on the beach. For the first time in weeks, the house was quiet and still. The production team had spent the last few days taking down a lot of the wires and lights and cameras and getting the place cleaned out. They were all getting packed up and set to get back to their real lives.

I found no peace in it at all. The girl I had fallen for was off somewhere with another guy, so I asked the guys on the crew for a favor:

Is there any way you can get me on a horse?

They graciously obliged. That was my saving grace that day. I got out on horseback and rode for hours, and my mind just wandered.

I had been sitting around beating myself over the head trying to figure out what was going on, but no matter how I looked at it, it racked my nerves. If I didn't leave here with Paige on my arm, I was going to be severely heartbroken; it would be a tough thing to overcome.

My heart was out on a limb, hanging by a thread, and Paige was the one in control of that thread. Not knowing whether it was going to be a happy or sad ending was really tough to deal with, tougher than I ever thought it would be.

I'd loved once before—put my whole heart out there—and it didn't work out, so I grew a steel coat over my heart and never put it back out on a limb. I had with Paige, though, and I'm thankful that I did because I'd definitely fallen in love with her. It was just going to devastate me if she didn't pick me.

If she picked me, it was going to be the most amazing thing ever, a blessing from above, something I'd prayed about for a long time. I'd been asking God to send me a beautiful, godly woman, inside and out, and if she picked me, I was going to be the happiest man on this Earth. I just wanted to take off for a whole solid month and lie around and kiss her until she just couldn't stand it anymore.

I told Paige that I'd give her forever, and I said that because I meant it. I opened my heart up to her and gave her all of it. I'd absolutely fallen in love with her.

You know, it was a wonderful feeling when she looked in my eyes and told me she was falling in love with me more and more each day. That's something that no one had ever said to me before—especially the way she said it to me. I didn't care if I sounded too sensitive because my feelings for her were real. If anybody wanted to say anything to me about being too sweet here, too bad. They had to get over it because these were my feelings toward her.

I'm a cowboy, you know? And I knew that when I got home I might hear some stuff from my buddies: "You put your heart out there on a limb. You shouldn't have done this—you shouldn't have opened up. You don't need to be sensitive. What's wrong with you?"

But at the end of the day, I didn't give a crap what they said because I'd be coming home to a beautiful woman that I'd fallen in love with, that I was hopefully going to raise a family with, so none of that stuff they might have said would have mattered. What mattered then was how I was feeling in my heart.

That's what went through my mind for a solid day. I was riding in the clear sunshine and thinking about how I was one step away from being the luckiest guy in the world.

When a cowboy's in a jam or doesn't know what to do, or when life throws you one of those unforeseen curves, there's a saying that usually applies, and it's a good motto to live by:

"Pull your hat down."

Normally you say, "Pull your hat down" when you're fixin' to go after a yearling in the pasture or rope a calf in the arena. If your hat's sitting high up on your head when you take off, it's gone. You're gonna lose it. So we say, "Pull your hat down" and get ready to take on whatever might be coming at you, that way you don't lose it.

It's like saying, "Poke your chest out and just get ready for it," something unpredictable is fixing to happen but you know something's coming and you better be ready for it.

I spent that day pulling down my hat.

The sun went down and I sat out on the beach by myself, just watching it sink. Somewhere right about then she was watching that sunset with someone else. But by then I was feeling good. I was going to get the sunset tomorrow—and hopefully many more. A day on horseback and all the fresh air had been good for me. That's where I belong.

I didn't hear Jeremiah when he got in. I slept right through it. I hadn't slept well in weeks, but that night I passed right out. I was excited for tomorrow.

I was finally going to get to take Paige back to the ranch.

13

THE SIMPLE BLESSINGS

It was another beautiful day. Gorgeous.

We met in the morning at the airport right by Dorgan's Inn where Paige was staying. The town of Fairhope where *Sweet Home Alabama* is filmed is about a four-hour drive from my ranch in Geneva, Alabama. I'm right along the Florida panhandle state line.

I've made the drive about a thousand times in my one-ton GMC dually. It has 240,000 miles on it (my other truck has 194,000 miles—I'm hell on equipment) and I've hauled horses and cattle up and back every county road in the state so many times I feel like I know every curve in those country back roads. Sometimes the bugs are caked so thick on the windshield it takes a chisel just to get a decent view down the damn road.

But today we were going there in style. Thanks to TV wizardry, there was a twin-engine private jet fueled and ready to go. Paige was waiting there on the tarmac for me. I made the long walk up to her, my spurs scraping the runway faster and faster as I got closer and closer. The four-hour drive was reduced to 35 minutes in the air, about 8,000 feet over the countryside. She was right next to me.

BUBBA:	I've been waitin' for this moment—I really have.
PAIGE:	Good.
BUBBA:	I'm glad to be on a plane with you goin' back to my place.
PAIGE:	Me too.
BUBBA:	I've been wantin' to show you ever since I met you, and, uh, I wish we could just stay there.
PAIGE:	[LAUGHS] I know
	[THEY KISS.]
BUBBA:	Well there's more to bein' a cowboy than just runnin' around chasin' cattle, ridin' horses, gettin' bucked off—that's the tough part about it. But what I've come to find out, the easy part about bein' a cowboy is throwin' that sensitive side out there. Working hard and also loving hard, you know? 'cause when I love, I love hard.

The plane touched down and within a few minutes we were walking up the front porch to the home I built in Geneva. It has all the basics, but it's in real need of a woman's touch.

We had joked around about the closet space she might need, and there's plenty of that to go around. I could see rows and rows of her boots lined up inside the closets I'd built. It's a modest house, but I know it can be a real home someday.

Oh, she's wearing the boots I bought for her on our last date. She remembered! That's good! Those boots look so good on her.

After a look around, we settled down on the front porch and poured some sweet tea. I confessed that a lot of days end with me sitting out here on this porch alone.

PAIGE: Well that's gotta be lonely.

BUBBA: Occasionally a buddy will come by, but they're nowhere near as pretty as you are.

PAIGE: [LAUGHS] I'll take that as a compliment.

BUBBA: Yeah, you better.

PAIGE: Your buddies. Thank you.

BUBBA: But you know, you bein' here right now, I feel like this is where you belong. I hope that's not too strong to say, but—

PAIGE: No, it's not, at all.

BUBBA: I'm really glad that you came into my life, I really am. You know, I couldn't be happier right now. I could win the world's biggest rodeo or ride the meanest, toughest bronc for eight seconds and it wouldn't matter. None of that would matter. What matters is this right here.

PAIGE: I agree. I couldn't be happier right now either.

BUBBA: You know, I don't know if you like rockin' chairs, but that's what's on the front porch.

PAIGE: I love rockin' chairs, and porches. [LAUGHS]

BUBBA: Rockin' chairs and—

PAIGE: And bein' with you. I love bein' with you.

BUBBA: You know, look how this is. This is what it would be.

From around the corner my mom came walking up with my nieces.

And I almost lost it right there.

Introducing a girl you've fallen for to your mom is a big moment. We were both choking back the tears. A mom can tell when it's for real. There's just no faking it.

MOM: You deserve somebody that's gonna be good to you and that's gonna be here.

BUBBA: The main thing is she stands behind me for what I do for a livin', you know? She's definitely the woman that I want to stay here with me. She loves camping. She loves anything outdoors, you know? And she likes to cook. And she also cooks everything with bacon grease, so we're gonna get along good.

MOM:	[LAUGHS] I like her already.
BUBBA:	I know you do. I knew you would. They asked me about it before. I said, "Listen, my mother'll read her over in two seconds and it'll be a no or a go."
MOM:	I've got a good feelin' about her. She's beautiful too.
BUBBA:	Absolutely gorgeous. She's just— she's definitely the woman that I want to stay here with me.
MOM:	I'm glad, hun. I just want you to be happy.
BUBBA:	I know you do.
MOM:	Somebody that's gonna be good to you and y'all are gonna have a life together, and ... I'm gonna get real sentimental here.
BUBBA:	The family and everything, you know? She told me—
MOM:	She's very much a family girl, and that's what you need, you know? You're family-oriented and if she is, it's a good combination.
BUBBA:	She told me that bein' around me makes her wanna be a better person, that's she's never met a better man than I am. And that means a lot. That's the nicest thing somebody's ever said to me, ever.

MOM:	Keep my fingers crossed.
MOM:	(To Camera) I'm gonna get choked up. I'm so happy for him 'cause he's happy. He's just bubbling inside. He's just—he's in awe, he's in awe with her. He said, "Mama, she is so real, inside and out." And that means everything, and she's very family-oriented. I know we all mean a lot to him and he means so much to us.
MOM:	Be yourself, be the good man that I know you are. You deserve the best. [HUGS BUBBA]
BUBBA:	I love you, Mama.
MOM:	I love you.
BUBBA:	You're the best, you know that?
MOM:	Bring her home. Bring her home. [LAUGHS]
BUBBA:	(To Camera) My mother told me, "You need to bring her home son." My mother has never, ever told me one time to bring anybody home, and that's just what I'm gonna do.
MOM:	Bring her home and be happy.

In the evening I took her out to the pasture near my home. There's a cowboy church out there that a few of us helped build. It started as a few of us under an oak tree, and from there we all built it up real nice, a small house of prayer. Right in front of it are some pens for keeping cattle and an arena for roping and riding. The arena's really popular with young kids around here. A lot of them come here to watch us ride and rope, and then that gets them interested to stay after and stick around the church. It's a great place to spend a Sunday morning, do some praying, and then get some riding in with the kids in the area.

I had a few dozen head of cattle over there, so we took some horses and mounted up and I let Paige do some riding with the herd. She knew just how to handle that horse and drive the cattle.

PAIGE:	Are we just gonna push 'em right across and hope they go in there?
PAIGE:	(To Camera) We're gonna push a bunch of cows. We're gonna move 'em across the pen, and this is what I enjoy doin'.
BUBBA:	I'm gonna let you take the tail-end, okay?
PAIGE:	Okay.
BUBBA:	If one takes off, just stay where you're at. Never leave the herd.
PAIGE:	Okay.
BUBBA:	(To Camera) The cattle start driftin', and she goes right around. She does her job.
PAIGE:	Hey, hey! [WHISTLES] Hey cow! [WHISTLES]
BUBBA:	(To Camera) She actually got out in front of me a little bit, which is what I like to see.
PAIGE:	Am I doin' good?
BUBBA:	Yes ma'am, yes ma'am.

BUBBA: (To Camera) She can ride a horse—
she really can. She's a definite
cowgirl.

PAIGE: Yay!

We took the horses over there underneath this old pecan tree, and
I had this little blanket laid out there with a little basket with
two wine glasses and a bottle of wine. I had a few flowers laid out
for her too. This was going to be our last evening together before
she had to make her final decision, and I wanted her to see how
romantic this cowboy could be.

BUBBA: You know, I'm not beatin' around the
bush about anything Paige. I really
do have major feelin's for you.

And, um, I really want you to be
with me, you know? And of course
I wanna be with you. I know you've
gotta make that decision. You gotta
do what's best for your heart, but I
just know there's a major connection
there, and I don't wanna spend
another night without you.

PAIGE: You're amazing. Ever since I first
talked to you, my feelin's have just
gotten stronger and stronger, and
like I said, you're not just everything
I wanna be with, you're everything I
wanna be, and you make me into a
better person.

BUBBA:	Well, I just know that I wanna get up every day and go to work and know that there's somebody back at home that I wanna support, and I want that person to be you.
PAIGE:	I wanna support you too, in everything, and I can be with a cowboy.
BUBBA:	I mean this'll be—whoa! [WHISTLES AT HORSES]

Our two American quarter horses snatched back from the tree and broke free from the ties to the tree branches. They both pulled back on the reins and shook and stomped until they got themselves untied and took off running. Maybe they were trying to get out of earshot of all this loving talk.

Paige reached over and grabbed my hand and squeezed it, and she said, "That's the most beautiful thing." And I agreed with her: It was beautiful. As we were sitting there loving on each other, the two horses took off running wide open across that pasture, and we just sat there and smiled and laughed at each other. It was absolutely amazing.

She said, "That was beautiful, Bubba."

"It's beautiful, but not as beautiful as you," I told her.

You know, it was beautiful to see these two horses just running off wild out in the pasture. One's a bay and the other one's a chestnut. They're full brothers, and they're absolutely the two most gorgeous horses in the state of Alabama right now. They can do it all. They can do ranch work, and you can back them up into the box to rodeo—run one, tie one and six if you need to, or team rope some steers, bulldog, whatever you need to do. And you can also take a little four-year-old child and throw him on the back of them and turn them loose. They're just awesome horses, broke to death.

Those horses respect me, and being a cowboy is all about demanding respect. I take pride in everything that I do. And I believe in signs. This was a very beautiful sign.

Two proud horses started running side by side in a full sprint back and forth across the pasture. They were in a full-on run, the pounding of their hooves shaking the ground and their heavy, deep majestic breaths were in unison as they kept perfect pace with each other. They looked like they were running 100 miles an hour, just gliding across the horizon.

By then the sun had set below the tree line, and the light was fading fast. The sky was turning dark purple and then blue, and the first stars were starting to show.

Watching two horses sprinting in perfect unison was the perfect example of the life I was imagining for myself: breaking free, living life at full speed, charging forward with nothing holding me back, knowing another soul was right there next to me, stride for stride.

PAIGE: There it goes.

BUBBA: That's the life that I can give you, you know? I'm just a cowboy that works hard all the time, and I'm good at what I do. That's somethin' I'm always gonna do is be a cowboy.

PAIGE: That's what I like about you.

BUBBA: Huntin', fishin', and doin' whatever you wanna do too, you know? Go out to eat, whatever you wanna do.

PAIGE:	By your side all the time. You'll take me everywhere.
BUBBA:	I promise you, and I'll never leave your side. You can always trust me, you know that.
PAIGE:	I do trust you.
BUBBA:	And I will always protect you, always.
PAIGE:	I know you will. [WATCHING HORSES RUN] Yeah, I knew it'd break. They're so pretty.
BUBBA:	That's okay, they'll be all right.
PAIGE:	We'll go catch 'em later. It'll be fun.
BUBBA:	Let 'em run. Let 'em run. Let 'em run wild.
PAIGE:	I don't mind goin' to catch 'em with you. I don't have a care in the world when I'm with you.
BUBBA:	Wild and free.
PAIGE:	It does, it makes me happy.
BUBBA:	They're havin' a good time.
PAIGE:	They are.
BUBBA:	Not as good a time as I'm havin'.
PAIGE:	Wild and free.
PAIGE:	But I can take care of myself, but I need you. I want you [LAUGHS]. I know you will.

BUBBA: You're a very strong-willed woman too, that's what I like about you. You really are. You're absolutely gorgeous, Paige.

PAIGE: Thanks, Bubba. You make me feel good. You're the only one that's taken care of me this whole time.

BUBBA: (To Camera) Just sit there, watchin' the sunset with Paige. It doesn't get any better than that, you know? I mean, she's the best woman I've ever met in my entire life.

PAIGE: What are you thinkin' now, right now? How are you gonna sleep tonight?

BUBBA: I'm gonna sleep okay because we had a wonderful time together today, and I showed you what I was all about, and I showed you where I want you to be in my life. Paige, I have definitely fallen in love with you, and I don't ever wanna spend another minute without you.

PAIGE: I've fallen in love with you too, Bubba. And I do more and more every day, especially when I'm with you. [KISS] Thank you for bein' so wonderful.

BUBBA: Darlin', you're the wonderful one, not me. [KISS] I don't wanna lose you. You hear me?

PAIGE:	I hear you. You can just feel the love between us. You've showed me everything a guy should be—a man should be—how you should treat somebody, what I should expect, and you've showed me that you've changed my mind about how I thought about guys.
BUBBA:	(To Camera) This is an absolute miracle, you know? The perfect sunset, the perfect night, and the perfect woman put on this Earth. This has just been the perfect day for me and, and I'm looking forward to many more perfect nights like this. She is the most wonderful lady I've ever met in my entire life.
BUBBA:	I have really fallen in love with you, Paige. And I don't wanna spend another minute without you. I want you by my side, the whole time.
PAIGE:	Me too.

We kissed goodbye—a slow, sweet kiss goodnight. It dawned on me that this was what I'd been waiting on my entire life.

And, Paige was it.

That was the most beautiful sunset I'd ever encountered with anybody. I knew that God had created that moment just for me. I'd been praying about this.

I was very thankful and feeling so blessed to have her in my life. I didn't know what I would do without her. It was a dream come true. I was ready to get down on one knee and propose to her. I wanted her to be my wife. I was going to do what my mother said and bring her back to the ranch.

It was every cowboy's dream, to come home to a beautiful woman, to spend a beautiful night with a beautiful woman like Paige. She was my dream come true.

As she walked away, I just stood there looking out at that deep purple sky for a moment.

Dreams

A lot of thought is given to someday meeting "the woman of your dreams".

In my experience there is only one thing more powerful than the woman of your dreams. And that's the woman that you're thinking about in those first few seconds when you wake up in the morning.

She might be someone you knew a long time ago. She might be a person you recently met. She might be a good friend that you wish were something more. Maybe it's a girl you see every day and hadn't thought much of it, but suddenly there she is, right in front of you, in those first few very quiet moments when your eyes are barely open.

This is the universe telling you who you should be with.

The only question is, what are you going to do today to make it happen?

Before every day gets complicated, it always starts out very simply. At least that's the way it is out here in the country.

It's usually real quiet around here. But even when you are jolted awake by a dog howling, or the neighbor doing a little target practice with a shotgun, my guess is we all have those first few moments to ourselves in some way.

I like to try to honor those instincts and visions and voices I have first thing.

The day is about to get busy and noisy. And if you aren't careful, it will make you forget that pure thought you had as your mind came alive today.

Who was the person on your mind at the very start of the day today?

To those of you who have this pure vision of that special woman, and then get to look over and see her right beside you every morning as the light shines through the window, well, you are the luckiest of us all.

14

KNOWING WHEN TO WALK AWAY

The next day we got ready for the finale.

Jeremiah and I had been separated from each other. We were put up in a hotel while the crew took all the rest of the equipment out of the mansion by the bay. The mansion was being changed back from a fraternity house to someone's real home again; a fresh coat of paint and it was like we weren't even there.

It was a long day of waiting around. How much of this journey was real? And how much was just a coat of paint away from being another washed-over memory? These friendships we all had made— my heart felt they were set in stone and would last a lifetime. My mind knew that maybe a lot of it was part of a television show. But mostly I focused on these feelings I was having for a girl.

I replayed everything that happened, over and over again. It was as real as anything I had ever experienced. Take a few weeks away from all of life's distractions—cell phones, the Internet, TV—and I think it's very human to turn your attention to the things that are most important in the world: friendships, and finding someone to share your life with.

I was convinced I had found both. There was only one more thing to be done: A cowboy always backs up his words with his actions, and that's part of the Cowboy Code as well.

That was the last place I ever thought I'd be—walking into a jewelry store, scraping together part of my life savings, and looking at diamond rings with a camera crew following along. I'd never bought a ring before, but it was the right thing to do in that moment. I knew it in my heart. I was ready to feel that way every day from then on.

Paige had been a "trophy" for the group of us to chase after these past four weeks. Some of the guys wanted very much to take that trophy home. Not me. I didn't want the "trophy." I wanted Paige. I wanted to be leaving and making Paige an honest woman. I had a short conversation with the jewelry store clerk:

BUBBA: I'm the one that's lucky. Bein' run over by 3,000 head of cattle seems a lot less scary than standin' in this jewelry store, pickin' out an engagement ring. Actually that ring right there says it, says it all right there. Let me have that one.

CLERK: Let's take a look at that one. It's a beautiful ring.

BUBBA: (To Camera) It is a beautiful ring. Paige is the only woman that's ever made me this nervous and ... and right now my heart is pounding. It feels like it's just gonna jump clean outta my chest, but it's also good in a way too because I've never felt this way about anybody.

The ring was small, but I think the message is what's important. It conveyed my feelings for her. If you decide to be with a cowboy, you might not get the biggest ring of all, but this cowboy was prepared to back that ring up with a lifetime of providing her with everything she needs. As I like to say from time to time, I may not die a rich man, but I'm gonna die a happy man, doing what I love to do.

I'm going to walk up to Paige at the finale, get down on one knee, and ask her to be my wife.

That moment was less than 24 hours away.

> BUBBA: (To Camera) The next time that I see Paige, I'm gonna have this ring in my pocket, and I'm ready to get down on one knee and make an honest woman out of her, give her everything that she ever wanted.
>
> CLERK: Here you are.
>
> BUBBA: That is beautiful, absolutely gorgeous.
>
> BUBBA: (To Camera) Marriage is a sacred commitment that two people have between each other, and I'm ready to have that commitment with Paige. She's a wonderful person and I'm ready to be married to her.
>
> BUBBA: That'll make her happy, guaranteed.
>
> CLERK: I'm sure it will.

More waiting, and then they film me getting dressed, which only took me a few minutes.

Black Stetson hat.

I'm good to go.

They ask me if I'm nervous. I won't lie. I've made it this far on honesty, there's no need to change it up now.

So I had a few more words for the camera people as the big moment approached. I told them how I truly felt:

BUBBA: (To Camera) You know, this morning I woke up and today is the day. Today is the day that Paige makes her decision and, ya know, I would be lyin' if I said I wasn't nervous. I'm very nervous right now 'cause I've just expressed my feelings, and I've fallen in love with Paige, and I don't … I don't want to be turned down.

Once you look into her beautiful brown eyes, I mean, all the … all those nerves just go away, you know? She's just got this calming personality about her, and I definitely am going to get lost in her brown eyes every day of my life.

I mean, she … you know … she has completely stolen this heart. I get twisted up.

She has definitely stolen my heart, you know? I mean, I'm just so excited. I'm … I'm blushing right now, you know? I'm nervous. My knees are a little weak, you know? I'm sweating to death even though it's 45 outside.

There's just no beating around the bush about it. I mean, she has got my heart. She makes me smile all the time, you know? I can't quit thinking about her. And I just … I never thought this would happen, and it has happened.

When Paige first showed up here, she told us all—there was 22 of us standing there—that she had been praying for a long time that she would find her soul mate, you know? That she had been through a lot of rough times and trials in her life, and when she said that, I thought, wow, that's … that's awesome because I've been doing the same thing, you know?

And, I've kind of had to keep my chin up, you know?

Sometimes my head goes down a little low, but, you know, I just prayed about it, that I'd find my true soul mate—somebody that I could raise a family with, fall just so deeply in love with that you don't ever want to be away from that person. And, she told me just a little while ago that her prayers had been answered. And the same for me too. I mean, the feeling is absolutely mutual. We have both been blessed and it doesn't get any better than this.

Bubba and Paige Thompson. I mean, that's got a beautiful ring to it, don't you think?

I have definitely fallen in love with Paige. When two people fall in love, you know, nobody else matters.

She said that her heart has been broken many a times by cowboys, you know? And, that every little girl dreams of growing up and marrying a cowboy and having kids, you know, and a family. And, she just looked at me and said, "But you're different.

"You're a real cowboy. I know you would never do anything to hurt me, and I know that I could always trust you."

I just sittin' here wonderin', you know, wonderin' what her emotions are, her feelin's. She told me last night, and I feel really good about 'em, you know? I mean, she's a wonderful person. I can't say that enough. I'm ... I'm ... I'm feelin' weird inside. It's a feelin' that I have never felt before. And, uh, and I like it but yet I'm kinda scared too, in a way.

The scary part is, uh, her not wantin' me. The scary part is her lookin' me in the face, tellin' me that she's fallin' in love with me and that she would love to do this—what I had showed her yesterday—love to be in the family with me, you know, and ... and do the type of work that I do, you know, and live in my house with me, and then, uh, her change her mind. That's the scariest thing.

I leaned over there and whispered in her ear and told her that, you know, whatever decision she makes is what she needs to do, you know? Just put it in God's hands. That I really do, you know, that I care about her and I ... I was just shootin' her straight.

I've only told one girl that I've fallen in love with her and it's a long time ago.

And, it was just puppy love, is what it was, you know? We dated for a while, but it didn't mean anything like this does. You know, this ... this is the real deal and, uh, and I hope it stays that way.

I'm rugged, ya know? I'm ready to take on anything. I never get nervous. If a horse has bucked me off six times, I'm gonna get back on him again and ride that seventh one out. He may buck me off but that's fine. I don't get nervous. It just ... it just doesn't happen, but today I'm nervous, ya know? Because I'm sittin' here waitin' her final decision and uh, it's got me scared.

I've been sittin' around beatin' myself over the head, tryin' to figure out what's going on, but uh, either way you look at it, it's just nerve-racking.

If I don't leave here with Paige on my arm, I'm gonna be severely heartbroken, ya know? It's gonna be a tough thing to overcome.

Ya know, right now my heart's out on a limb. It's hanging by a thread and Paige controls my feelings right now, whether they're gonna be happy feelings at the end or ... or sad feelings, so, ya know, it's just, it's really tough to have to deal with. I didn't ever think it would be this tough.

Ya know I'd, I'd loved once before. I put my whole heart out there, and it didn't work out, so, ya know, I kinda—I had a steel coat grow over my heart and I never put it back out on a limb. But I have with Paige and I'm thankful that I did, and I've definitely fallen in love with her and I'm ready to spend the rest of my life with her.

It's just gonna devastate me if she doesn't pick me.

I sure don't wanna get the gate.

And I will love her until the end of time.

I'm one step closer to walking away with the love of my life.

I ... I told Paige that I would give her forever, and I said that because I mean it.

By then I was being whisked from the hotel where we were holed up, over the hilly drive that is Baldwin County State Road 32. It swells up and down, past gorgeous ranches and farms and perfectly framed, long wooden fencing along the roadside. The weather had turned colder in our month there, and the trees were auburn. The fields looked a little bare, like they were bracing for a blast of winter. Around here the winters are just short and cold enough to put you in the spirit, and then the hot summer in those pastures is waiting a few short weeks away.

We were getting closer and then the car pulled to the side of the road.

Like all the people on the television crew, the driver had one of those secret service earpieces in his ear, and he was talking to someone. Maybe the only thing that can make you more paranoid than people talking about you behind your back is people talking in code about you on radios right in front of you.

"In position," the driver said.

"Copy that," he said a few moments later.

Did all the people on that radio frequency already know how this was going to end? Was I going to be the last person to know? It was all surreal.

I started looking for clues in everything. Did the wardrobe person put me in a specific color because I was the "winner" and it would look better with Paige's dress? These were the little tricks the mind plays on you when you are living half in captivity, and half on top of the world.

They finally took me to a dressing room inside the house, but the wait would be hours.

I was listening for every sound. Every footstep over a tree root got my mind racing. "Is that Jeremiah? Is he going first? Am I second to see her? Does that mean he's been chosen? Or me?"

To be honest I was happy these things were crossing my mind. They were survival instincts. It was nice to have them sharpened and at the ready. It was a reminder that I still had my senses about me and hadn't taken a full leave of reality.

I didn't have all that much to say, and I hadn't planned anything out—other than to have a ring in my jacket pocket. And I only triple-checked that about a hundred times.

There was a knock on the door.

"Just a few more minutes," the voice said.

"You bet," I said.

I was in our old room. There must have been 12 guys sleeping there in bunks a few weeks ago. Now it was all restored to a plush, comfortable, well-appointed, proper Southern bedroom. It looked like the honeymoon suite in a vintage bed and breakfast. There was a mirror in the corner.

I took a last look and pulled down my hat.

It was cold outside, and I could see my breath condensing in front of me. I was following a production person around the side of the house, and he had a flashlight leading the way, making sure we didn't trip over the maze of wires and cables snaking their way around the property. It was pitch dark out and the sky was full of stars.

We walked closer to the driveway where Paige was waiting.

It looked like a pathway to heaven.

My goodness was all I remember thinking.

It was a scene from out of a fairy tale. The driveway was lit up with globes of soft light and every tree twinkled with Christmas lights. Lanterns hung along the side of the old dirt road. It was all lit up so bright you could have landed a 747 right there. The trees were bright orange, red, and dark green and her dress was white.

It was a fairy-tale setting.

Would I be riding off at the end with the princess, or was I the guy who was destined to fall on his sword?

She was standing at the end of the drive looking down the lane.

And in that instant, when I met her brown eyes from about 50 yards away under the bright lights, I knew two things for certain:

I was absolutely blessed, and right, and destined to fall in love with her ... and I was going to be leaving here heartbroken and alone.

What happened next felt like a blur.

BUBBA:	Oh, my God, gorgeous.
PAIGE:	Hey, Bubba.
BUBBA:	Hey.
PAIGE:	How are you doin'?
BUBBA:	I'm good. How are you?
PAIGE:	Good, give me a hug.
BUBBA:	Don't say anything.
PAIGE:	Okay.

BUBBA: I just wanna look into your eyes for a minute. Your eyes are beautiful Paige, but they don't lie. I know your heart lies with Jeremiah, and I'm okay with that because what matters most is that you're happy, you know? If your heart belongs to him, that's fine.

Inside I was numb, and I think it was taking most of my energy to just keep standing up straight. I was angry and hurt all over. Inside I just kept looking to take the high road.

BUBBA: You know the other day, we were sittin' in that field and I told you that, I said a word that I never said before, which is *forever*. You know, I meant it then, I still mean it now, you know? And after this decision, you know, a part of me will always love you forever. I'll always hold a special place in my heart for you. You're a wonderful woman and I don't think I'll ever find another one just like you. With this decision, you know, it's tough on me but like I said, I'll always love you.

PAIGE: You—

BUBBA: No matter ... don't ... don't, it's okay. It's all right. It's all right.

PAIGE: I'm sorry.

BUBBA:	It's okay. It's totally fine. I'm a cowboy. I'm good. I can handle it. What matters most is that you're okay.
PAIGE:	I love you too, Bubba. I do. I do.
BUBBA:	I know you do. I know you do.
PAIGE:	I do, I promise. You're the greatest guy I've ever met, and I don't know why my heart can't feel what my mind tells me to.
BUBBA:	That's okay, that's totally okay, sweetie. That's totally okay.
PAIGE:	I wish it could. I've prayed to God about it. It's like, the perfect man's here, why can't I feel it?
BUBBA:	If God's in you, you know, who can be against you? Okay?
PAIGE:	I'm so blessed to have met you and you're gonna be in my life forever.
BUBBA:	Absolutely, absolutely.
PAIGE:	You are. I do love you.
BUBBA:	I know.
PAIGE:	I do.
BUBBA:	I know you do.
PAIGE:	And He does too.
BUBBA:	I know He does.
PAIGE:	I'm sorry.
BUBBA:	Don't worry about it. [HUG]

PAIGE:	I love you, Bubba. I do.
BUBBA:	There's nothin' to be sad about.
PAIGE:	[WEEPS] I'm sorry I hurt you.
BUBBA:	You're okay darlin'. You're all right. You got the love of your life waitin' for you. You hear me? It's all right.
PAIGE:	I'm sorry I hurt you.
BUBBA:	You're all right. You're all right.
PAIGE:	I am.
BUBBA:	You're all right. Okay.
PAIGE:	Thank you.
BUBBA:	All right, darlin'.
BUBBA:	(To Camera) You know, walkin' up there and seein' Paige tonight, I knew that that ring was gonna stay in my pocket. I knew that her heart didn't belong to me. Bein' here, goin' through this, it just reassures me that my American dream will come true, you know? There is a beautiful woman out there waitin' on me and, uh, I hadn't found her yet but, I'm gonna find her soon.
BUBBA:	I'll always love you, even if it's from far away.

I had learned to love my son from far away all these years. My son had taught me a lot about keeping someone in your heart and prayers, and taking them with you wherever you go. It was sad, but it gave me strength to think of it in that moment.

I turned and walked away.

I looked over my shoulder for a moment on the way out. And lowered my hat as I walked off.

PAIGE:	Bye.
BUBBA:	Bye.
BUBBA:	(To Camera) It's a kick in the gut. This old cowboy, he's gonna pull his hat down and he's gonna ride another day. Nothin's gonna hold me down, I can promise you that.

I didn't get the girl.

My mind was racing with the question ... why? What had I done wrong? I'd put my whole heart on the line, and instead she chose someone who was aloof, unsure, and somewhat distant. I was ready to make the ultimate commitment, and he wasn't.

I had no trouble speaking from the heart. He was strained and unsteady. But she fell for him instead of me.

Was there a lesson in it? Had I played it all wrong? Do women really want "games"? Do they want to keep guessing, instead of being reassured of your genuine intentions?

After thinking it over for all of five minutes I settled on an answer. I'm a straight shooter. That's the cowboy way. That's what I am going to continue to strive to be.

If there was a lesson in it, it was this: You ride hard, you work hard, you love hard. But you have to know and believe there is a higher plan, and it doesn't always include riding off into the sunset on every deal.

Garth Brooks might have summed it up best when he said, "Some of God's greatest gifts are unanswered prayers."

One thing about being on a television show like this was I'd already agreed that I wouldn't tell anyone anything about it. Normally I would have called up my mom, or my friends, and looked for a sympathetic ear. In this case, I'd signed a contract saying I was going to have to deal with the fallout from everything I'd been through and not say a word about it to another soul.

A lot of the people on the TV crew had become my good, trusted friends. And the finale night was also their night to have a party to wrap things up. They invited me along and that took a lot of the sting out of the rejection. Though I will admit, while we were having some laughs and throwing back a few cold ones, it hurt to think that at that moment Paige was alone somewhere, moving forward with another guy.

Broken Hearts

When someone leaves you or moves on, they take a piece of your heart. The question is, how can you get it back?

He or she has it. And there are a lot of times it feels like they outright stole it. They have something that's yours.

Your heart is wounded. There is a void that you feel.

For the longest time, no matter what you're doing or where you are, your mind is on that person. It is your body and soul searching for that missing piece of your heart.

It will look at your inbox every ten seconds, as if a message or text from her will somehow replenish the emptiness you feel. You will click on his or her facebook page a hundred times in a row, as if seeing a new post or photo or status is somehow going to give you the information you need to recapture the part of you that's gone missing.

All the weeks, or months or years you gave to him or her are gone. All the nice things you did, are unappreciated and those memories now turn on you, and twist you from the inside.

This is what happens when someone leaves you with a broken heart. And here is my policy on it – the cowboy way to break apart from someone when you no longer love them *is to ensure that the other person does not walk away with this feeling.*

There are enough ways you can tell someone they are appreciated, and cared for, and the memories you have together are treasured, and they are still loved, but you have another plan for your life.

It isn't difficult to find an end to a relationship that is caring and positive. It really isn't that hard of a thing to do.

If the other person didn't have enough compassion, and sense, and decency to move apart in the nicest way possible, it means they weren't a compassionate person to begin with.

There are some people who think the sun rises and sets on them every day. The first step is recognizing that the ex of yours who is making you feel this way is that type of selfish person.

If you were still together, you would be spending the rest of your life pouring quarters into a slot machine that just takes and takes, and rarely, if ever, pays out. That's just a sucker bet. Not one of us would play that type of game, and keep on throwing in more and more.

So recognize that every time you let a *"I wish she were here right now"* or *"if I lose 10 pounds and he sees me in a bikini on instagram he will regret it"* type of thought ruin another God-given moment, just think of that rotten, crooked slot machine ripping you off of your hard-earned cash.

But back to that most important thing – that piece of your heart that is missing *right now.*

Your body and soul are built to go look for it. It is only natural that they put out every feeler they have, and instruct you several times every second to get out there and find their lost basket of emotions and loving energy.

Some say you never get that piece of your heart back. That the love you gave was a gift, and though it may be unrequited or unappreciated, that was your gift and you can't have it back.

I'm not so sure I see it that way. I think you can get it back, and faster than you think.

You have to re-program yourself a little bit. Remind those loving places inside you that what they are missing is the sense of happiness – what they are *not* missing is that particular person.

Unwrap all those feelings from that person who has gone off. Remember, he or she just took their love and yanked it off the table, and left you without the caring to make sure you are OK. They left. They did not care.

As unfair as it feels, they didn't have the compassion to find a fair, and kind way to end the relationship.

They did not take the high road, with your heart in the balance.

Remind your body and soul of these facts. They are right to search for the love. But sometimes they confuse the person who has left, for the love you need to feel.

Assign a mental dead end sign, and soon your brain will refocus.

Away from that cheating, crooked, non-fulfilling slot machine that only knows how to take. And toward the happiness you really deserve.

A piece of your heart is gone. But remember this -- that piece *does not belong* to the person who rode off with it.

It will come back to you. It will find its way home.

It will be in better shape than ever, when the right, caring, compassionate, sweet, truly loving person comes into your life.

15

UNANSWERED PRAYERS

Unanswered prayers. The unanswered prayers were answered a few months later, when *Sweet Home Alabama* started airing on television.

And I started hearing from many of you.

It was surreal to see the events of a month playing out on the TV screen. The drama that we all felt—the arguments, the blood, sweat, and tears—seeing that all unfold on television was every bit like living it all over again. It felt like I was there again: the things that made me frustrated and upset, the feeling of being corralled from place to place. I hated Shaun Bigos all over again from the start, and then found myself liking him more and more as the weeks went by on TV.

But mostly, of course, it was hard to watch myself falling for Paige all over again. I had thought about her every day for the month or so since the night she turned me away, and then it started to fade. I'd think about her eight times a day, then seven. It felt good to be down to once or twice.

Then the TV show started airing and I started feeling all of those feelings of being attracted to her, and then drawn to her, and then falling for her, and finally in love with the girl. No sooner had I begun to get myself out of the woods than here I was right back in it again. And I didn't know who to talk to about it.

By now people were starting to see me all over town and asking me, "Does she pick you? I know she does!"

I couldn't let on any sign one way or the other. As much as I wanted to go to my mom or my nieces to talk it all out, I had given my word that I wouldn't tell a soul how it all ended up until after it aired on television. I don't play a lot of poker, but I put up a pretty good poker face on the outside for all those weeks. On the inside it was somewhat of a different story.

Every week would roll around and each new episode would come on the screen. I was a mixture of nervous, excited, and a little sick to my stomach. I knew I was about to hear myself drabble on and on about the girl I had fallen for. It was like watching yourself running head first into a concrete wall or somethin'. I'd find myself talking back to the screen, saying to that guy in the hat, "Don't do it! Turn around and run. This ends in disaster!"

But like I was in quicksand or something, I'd see myself falling deeper and deeper into it every week, with no chance for escape.

And then something wonderful happened that changed my life in a more meaningful way than I'd ever really imagined—I started hearing from many of you.

I'd never had a Facebook or Twitter account before, but a few weeks after the TV show first went on the air, I got myself one of each. So many of your emails and tweets and posts were so wonderful to me. They really lifted my feelings and spirits beyond anything I could imagine.

I don't want to repeat them here, but among my favorites were messages from people saying "thank you" for portraying someone from the South that has our values and believes in God. There were many times after walking away that I felt like I was the "loser" in the whole thing. I've never really felt good about finishing in second place, to be honest with you. But when people started recognizing little things that are important to me, like saying grace before a meal, or the way I talk about the values we are raised with down here, well, that made me feel like I'd accomplished what I set out to do on a whole other level.

As for Paige, I wish her well. But I don't think about her in that way anymore. I look back on it all and can see that there was a different plan for us.

I'm still out there in the pasture, riding alone.

Just the other day the guys and I were chasing down this old bull that had been hiding from us in some thick woods. The other guys spotted him and yelled, "Get after him, Bubba!" My horse took off at full speed and I came around the corner ready to rope him, and then, for no reason at all, that horse just stopped short and bogged his head, throwing me forward out of the saddle like a lawn dart. He lawn-darted me right into the rocks, and I hit the ground like a drunken sailor or something. The side of my head got all cut up, and my ear was about torn off the side of my head, and for a moment there I thought I broke my neck. I was out cold, just lying there on the ground.

But I was all right. After a few minutes I dusted myself off and got back up there and finished out the day's work. I come home at night pretty beat up and worked to the bone a lot, and I still imagine having a lovely woman there to spend the evenings with and start a family with.

Where will I find her? Of course, there's no way to know for sure, but I can tell you one place I will not find her for sure.

On television!

I decided right after this all ended that being a TV bachelor just isn't for me. It would probably be a whole lot of fun, and what guy doesn't dream of being around 20 or so beautiful women and going on dream dates every night?

But I just don't want to do it—mostly because I don't want to have to look any young lady in the eye and disappoint her after she's shown feelings for me the way I showed feelings for Paige.

I've already reached a good deal of my goals except for finding a woman to spend the rest of my life with that supports me whatever I do. That's kind of a hard situation because a lot of girls like the idea of a cowboy, but they don't like what comes with it. And so my goal is to find somebody to share my life with like that. And to finish my house and just keep decorating my place. You know—just live the good life.

The good life for me is living in the country. Weekends spent at the family cookouts. Doing a little traveling. Spending time with people that you love. Raising and training horses, and having tons of cattle to look after. That's the good life to me.

My definition of success is having your bills paid each month, and having groceries in the pantry and food on the table when you get home at night. It's also having a vehicle to drive and a roof over your head.

I'm not a materialistic person. I still drive a 1999 truck that I bought right when I was fresh out of high school. It's an old beat-up white pickup truck; both door handles on the inside are ripped out, so you have to reach outside to get out of the truck.

I also have a blue dually truck that hauls my trailer. I'd eventually like to get a new vehicle, but I'm not a materialistic type of guy, and I'm pretty rough and rugged with everything, so if I had something super nice at the ranch, chances are I'd probably have it messed up in a few weeks.

Well, I guess it would be nice to have tons and tons of dollars in the bank to go do what you wanted to do, travel here and travel there, but that stuff doesn't really interest me. I always want to be ahead, but coming home to my house at nighttime, enjoying my animals and my family and the house that I built, and riding up and down the dirt road in my old pickup truck is what matters to me the most.

Another goal I have is that I want to do something special for one of the most special women in my life, the one that taught me everything, my mom. She's always had a rough time, and my goal is to—one day soon—build her her own house. Right now, it's actually a major goal for me, in front of everything else. She deserves it—she made me a good man. I feel like it's the least I can do to repay the favor.

Imagine It, Then Say It.

One of the best things about our imaginations is, they are capable of perfection.

They often create the perfect night, the perfect setting, and the perfect special someone right there beside you.

In your imagination, you have no trouble telling her how happy you want to make her, how beautiful she is, how wonderful you feel whenever you are around her. In your imagination you tell her how talented and bright she is, and how she inspires you.

Usually these visions I get has her giving me a look, where she's so admiring, happy, impressed, and proud.

I love you is very easy to say, when you are imagining yourself with her.

It's doing it in real life where the issues all get in the way.

Let that imagination of yours go for a few moments and it all comes together!

Maybe it's you intercepting the ball and running it back down the sidelines, leaping over tackles and strong-arming your way into the end zone with time ticking down, and she's that beautiful cheerleader right there along the sidelines.

I'm doing this for you, you think, as you look over and catch her eye.

You're out on the beach on a clear night and fireworks are going off right above you, as you lean in for a soft kiss.

You are so beautiful to me, you can't help but say in the moment.

If there's one thing I have learned over the past few months, it's that we have more control to make these moments come true than we ever have. These visions that we are getting are like our little voice, corralling us in the right direction, where we are meant to be.

OK – not very many of us are actually going to score the winning touchdown in front of a crazed hometown crowd.

But lay out a blanket on a 50-yard line sometime when no one else is around, bring her a flower, and tell her she's the one who inspires you every day – and if she's the right one, she will appreciate the sincerity of the moment. It should mean more to her than a touchdown ever will.

The thing is, we don't say it.

We save it, thinking the moment has to be just right and the stars all have to be lined up.

Or even worse, we chicken out.

In those moments – all I can say is you have to *cowboy up*.

You might get bucked off but it won't sting you nearly as long as the regret you'll feel by shying away, and losing that girl to someone else.

We all come into these things with issues, and doubts. But I don't care what has happened to you in the past. Whether you were raised with nothing at all or spoon-fed and spoiled with fancy things from Tiffany since the time you were born.

This is your future, and when it comes to sharing your heart, you have to cowboy up and show some guts, and resolve, and heart. Be the strong, straight-shooting cowboy you were meant to be.

And women, this stuff doesn't come so easy for us. When your guy gives this a shot, you need to support him. Or he will be that reclusive colt, the one who flinches every time someone new comes around to the emotions he has tucked away.

For me, my imagination really gets the best of me at the end of a long day. I'll be riding back to my place. The sun will start going down at the top of the hill on the West side of the pasture.

I have done my fair share of imagining at that time of day. For me, it's always been a vision of a strong woman standing out by the barn as I am riding home. The wind is kind of blowing and it's a little dusty but she's there clean and pretty. I can't really see her face or the color of her hair, but I can feel her smiling at me from 400 yards away.

She's proud of me for working hard, and the house we've built, and I am driven to helping to build a better life for us.

How was your day?, I can't wait to ask her.

And I can almost hear her soft voice and see her face, and then I snap back to reality.

And there I am just riding home after another long day.

Cowboys get to see a lot of sunsets.

Next time I feel myself falling for a special lady, I am going to say everything that is in my heart. I am not holding anything back. I am going to do everything in my power to create those special moments, not just wait for them to come along. She's going to get all of me.

I don't want to see any more beautiful sunsets all alone.

16

Happy Endings

I met a married couple during my time on *Sweet Home Alabama* that you never get to see on screen. They own the giant Southern mansion where Paige lives in the show, and their story is inspiring.

Their names are Bill and Patty Dorgan, and the home they built is called The Dorgan's Inn.

As the story goes, Billy became successful by owning a bunch of doughnut shops all across the South. He spent the better part of 60 years up before the sunrise, opening those stores, going from one shop to two, to several dozen. He's a self-made man who built his fortune the old-fashioned way. And he'll tell you that all those years working hard like that kept him away from his family a lot, and he had to sacrifice a lot to get where he is. Now that he's made his mark on the world, what do you suppose he's doing with all the riches?

He built a beautiful home with his wife, Patty. Every floorboard is perfectly molded, every rooftop shingle perfectly crafted. It's the ideal Southern mansion, right on the water in Point Clear. Two long piers stretch out into the bay, each railing perfectly sanded, each plank evenly laid. The end of that pier might be the most serene spot I've ever been to. You can truly look out and see forever.

On the property right next to them, they built a house for all their kids and grandkids to be nearby. And then, to share it even further, they open their home to couples who want to get married, inviting them to spend the weekends there, getting married by the water as the sun sets. Each week during the summer months, Billy and Patty welcome in a new family and get to share in their love story. They are gracious hosts in the truest traditions of Southern hospitality.

A team of gardeners is out there on the grounds every day, but Billy is right there with them, wearing a safari hat. Each of those flower beds gets treated with care. At any moment someone from *Southern Living* magazine could show up, and this home would be ready for the cover.

Billy always calls his wife by her proper name, "Miss Patty." He has a nice sport-fishing boat moored at the marina down the street, which he uses to take guests out fishing in Mobile Bay. What did he name that dream yacht? *The Striker? The Southern Comfort? The Sea Dream?*

Of course, he named it *Miss Patty*.

But the most beautiful part of the Dorgan's Inn is what you might get to see if you are hanging around in the evenings. Then you'll see the man and wife of the house, in their later years, walking up and down the piers, still holding hands. And as the sun sets, they sit side by side on the rocking chairs on their front porch, holding hands and smiling at each other.

You can see them there, and feel the aura of two people counting their many blessings in life. Highest on that list? They found each other and stood by each other in struggles and in the good times as well. I didn't exactly find true love in *Sweet Home Alabama*, but I did find friendship and inspiration.

I believe we all have many blessings to be thankful for, and the more time we spend thinking about them and honoring them, the more we will attract that final link so many of us are missing in our lives—the special person to come home to, that special person to share our blessings with.

I want to run the ranch until I'm 75 years old with a beautiful wife and tons of kids and grandkids running around. That's my American dream. I want to live off the land, not struggle, and just get by.

I want to have a good, godly family. That's also my American dream. And I'm living three-quarters of that right now. I'm needing to find that other quarter to put the woman right there.

This is the code I choose to live by, a code of thankfulness, forgiveness, humility, working hard, and also loving hard; a code that tells us in each and every decision to seek to find the high road, in life and in relationships.

Everything happens for a reason. And remember, if, by chance, things don't go your way … don't let that stop you from fighting the good fight. Just pull your hat down and cowboy up.

You deserve all the love in the world.

That is my sincere wish, for all of you.

God Bless,
Bubba Thompson

APPENDIX

The Cowboy Code

In the mid 1940s the great cowboy singer/movie star Gene Autry created a Cowboy Code of moral, ethical, and patriotic traits every cowboy should live by.

The following are the original traits of that Cowboy Code and my interpretation of how I think they apply to love and relationships.

1. **The Cowboy must never shoot first, hit a smaller man, or take unfair advantage.**
   The cowboy must never take unfair advantage of a woman.

   There are times when a woman in your life is in need or distress and turns to you. She's wounded emotionally, like when she's coming straight out of a broken relationship and needs a shoulder to cry on. You should just be that shoulder to cry on, not the one that wants to lay down with her that night and take advantage of her.

   When a girl's an emotional wreck or has had a rough time with something in a relationship, she's at her weakest point. She's vulnerable and a lot of men will prey on that and that's just not the right thing to do. I mean, you're supposed to be a man, but if you're going to be a man, be a man. Stand up for what's right and take care of her, listen to what she needs to say.

Don't try to take advantage of her and use her. Don't prey on her because she's weak right now. That's just not the right thing to do.

2. He must never go back on his word, or a trust confided in him.

He must speak the truth to a woman, never betray her trust, and back up words with proper actions.

Whenever you tell somebody something or tell a woman something—you tell her today, "I'm gonna take you out Friday night"—you better make sure you got your plans lined up to do that. It may seem like something small, but there are feelings involved and more importantly, it's a trust thing.

You're responsible for keeping her feelings in your heart and in your mind and keeping them to yourself. You shouldn't go around telling everybody about it; don't tell her business to other people.

When she trusts you, she confides in you, and once you break that trust or lose that trust with somebody, that's something you can't ever get back.

When you lose that trust with somebody, you may be able to hang around them, spend a little bit of time with them, but they're not ever going to fully, completely trust you with anything once they've been disappointed.

3. He must always tell the truth.

You can't tell somebody what they want to hear just to make them feel better. Eventually the truth comes out.

Sometimes a woman might not want to hear what you have to say. You may have bad or upsetting news for her about how you feel. But the right thing to do is to be honest.

My grandfather always told the truth because if you didn't, there were going to be consequences. You didn't ever want to lie. And once you tell one lie, before you know it, you've got to say six more to cover up the first one that you told. That was always something bred into me—to always tell the truth.

This goes back to a man's word. It really is all you have—a man's word and a man's handshake.

In the instance where I might have something unpleasant to say to a woman, I just go ahead and tell her. It's not fair to lead someone on, let the relationship get that much stronger for the other person, and then all of a sudden drop the bomb on the other person.

Better to get the truth out there earlier. It's better to just tell them straight up, straight forward because it's going to hurt their feelings worse later on down the road.

4. **He must be gentle with children, the elderly, and animals.**
A woman is like a beautiful diamond. She should be treasured and appreciated, admired for her brilliance. You have to take care of her, cherish her, and love her.

She's a jewel. She's a gem; something special.

Women are special people. Ladies, they're amazing creatures. I mean that's what we are, creatures. And they just always need to be taken real good care of.

5. He must not advocate or possess racially or religiously intolerant ideas.

In addition to that, he must treat women with respect and equality.

I think a woman's place is right beside the man—not in front of him and not behind him, but right beside him. And I think that goes back to compromise. You both need to talk things out and try to compromise when you disagree.

6. He must help people in distress.

We're supposed to help each other out when people are having a rough time.

That goes back to just being a good neighbor and a good friend, whether it's on the side of the road with a tire blown out or being a shoulder to cry on.

You always have to help your neighbor. That's what life is about—helping each other out. So many people have forgotten that these days.

Men do need to be that knight in shining armor for a woman, whether she's their wife or their friend. They need to not always expect something in return.

7. He must be a good worker.

He must be a provider.

This isn't about money. It's about providing a woman a relationship where she can feel safe and secure.

Cowboys always feel better about doing the little things—fixing things around the house, doing errands and chores—when women reward them and tell them how much it's appreciated.

We're hard workers—we're bred for that. We'll get up tomorrow and do it all over again. So if a woman wants to keep her man, she better make sure he feels appreciated.

8. He must keep himself clean in thought, speech, action, and personal habits.

A cowboy always has to have an image to set for himself.

We always just try to dress appropriately, even if we're going to work out through the chute and get bloody and nasty and cut the bulls and do whatever we need to do. Our motto is to dress like you're making $100 a minute even if you're losing $200 a minute. So that's the way we always try to look presentable.

We always have our shirts tucked in. We always try to be clean-shaved. If you're not clean-shaved, at least be trimmed up nice. Have a nice haircut.

Always take your hat off when you walk inside or sit at the table. Just have manners. Always look presentable, smell nice, and try to look your best at all times.

That goes a long way. Women notice that and they want a nice, respectful man, someone who respects himself enough to stay cleaned up and presentable.

Women need to let men know that that's what they expect; they need to let 'em know that they're classy and they want classy men.

Men should always open the door. And if you're walking down the sidewalk, you need to be standing on the roadside—just for protection. The man's a protector. He always needs to protect you from all the elements, be it the weather or a car driving down the road.

You have to be a protector.

9. He must respect women, parents, and his nation's laws.

A woman should never take any less than what she deserves. That pretty much sums it up.

10. The Cowboy is a patriot.

You need to be a leader. You can say I'm a patriot out at the ranch. You kind of have to lead everybody. Even if you're the low man on the totem pole, hold your shoulders back and make decisions like you are a leader, and you will become one.

Today, in addition to the real patriots who go out and selflessly fight and sacrifice for our freedoms, a patriot is also someone who treats others as he or she would hope to be treated in return, and who thinks of their neighbors not just themselves.

Shaun Bigos

Here is a story with a wonderful ending for you.

I asked Shaun if it would be ok if I shared this with you all and he assured me it would be alright.

When our television show began to go on the air, Shaun began to hear it from a lot of people down South who were ready to deck him for some of the things he had said about us.

Calling people hillbillies and stupid, dirty and drunk will get you knocked out cold.

The comments he received ranged from people praying for his soul, to those telling him to go to hell, and some even sent him death threats.

Shaun tried to laugh it off and pretend it didn't bother him, and he got in some nasty twitter back and forths with people. But in this day and age it has to bother you if some nutcase out there sends you a nasty note. As much as Shaun tried to laugh it off in that deep husky voice of his – it bothered him.

It bothered all of us.

When people react like that, with hatred or threats, all it does is reinforce negative stereotypes about us here in the South. It is uncalled for.

As the weeks went on and the story played out on TV, people at home started to see what all of us got to see –

a guy who came in hard-headed having his heart opened up by our way of life.

As the weeks went by, a lot of people who had sent him nasty messages reached out again and apologized for their inappropriate remarks. That is the Southern way.

Meanwhile behind the scenes something else was going on.

A lot of young ladies watching up there in New York City were taking a very strong liking to that bad boy routine Shaun was flaunting on TV.

When he wasn't reading death threats, apparently he also had quite a few, shall we say, rather forward offers to come meet young ladies who were eager to meet him.

This went on for a few weeks and – from the way he describes it – Shaun's social calendar was pretty booked up.

As he started lightening up on TV, and embracing the South, in addition to the emails and texts from NYC, messages started coming in from across the country. Being the shipping logistics expert he is, Shaun categorized the messages, put them on a map, and planned himself a road trip to meet some of these young ladies in person.

His first stop was in Phoenix – to see a young woman who had emailed him a rather interesting message.

She was an oral surgeon, and had noticed while watching a scene where the two of us were roping in the yard, that Shaun was moving his jaw in a strange way that might cause him problems down the line.

All of us watched him run his mouth and threatened to break his jaw. Here this lady was noticing it might need to be fixed.

So off he went, not looking for any romance per se, but taking her up on a free consultation.

From there he would make his way across the Southwest to meet a slew of his female admirers.

One look, and the rest of that trip was cancelled.

Having dated so many women in the weeks prior, when Shaun laid eyes on her, he knew she was the one.

It reminds me of the Rascal Flatt's lyric, *"God Bless the broken road that led me straight to you."*

A few days later they flew back to New York together to gather up his stuff and move it down to Scottsdale.

On the long drive across the open ranges and American countryside, they decided to take a detour.

They made a stop in Las Vegas, and got married.

Shaun gave up smoking and drinking and is hopelessly in love.

As for the hair gel and the body waxing, well, let's just say there's some habits that are hard to break.

He moved far away from that concrete jungle, and lives in a place that's city enough for him, but also has the feel of the country.

And a year after they got married, he met the next love of his life – a beautiful baby girl.

So maybe it is possible to go on a dating show, and find true love, after all.

Questions from You

Over the course of writing this book, I have received countless emails and thousands of questions from all over. They helped me form what you've just read in this book, and I hope that I've helped many of you answer your questions. I wish I could answer each and every one of them here, but for now I will stick with answering just a few directly. My answers aren't the full solution to anyone's problems, but I wanted to at least give a short-and-sweet version of my thoughts on the questions that so many of you are asking.

Shyanne says:
> *I am dating a cowboy who is not treating me right, and what I mean by that is that all he does is accuse me of cheating when I'm not. I just don't know what to do anymore.*

Shyanne, I don't really have advice for you. I'm just going to tell you how it is. Your boyfriend probably accuses you of cheating on him all the time because of his own guilt. A lot of people let their guilt ruin their relationships, and if he's doing that, he's not being fair to you at all.

Normally what happens is that somebody feels guilty about something they've done, and they try to bring it down on you to make themselves feel better about what they did. That way they don't feel so bad about what they did to you.

Either he needs to let you go or you need to let him go. You don't deserve to be put on a guilt trip—no woman does. Pick yourself up, pull your hat down, and go on without him because there's someone out there that will treat you like you deserve to be treated.

Brittany asks:

> *My grandma always says that when it seems too good to be true, it is, but what's the difference between a good thing and too good to be true?*
>
> *... Being born and raised a country girl and now a single mom, I HAVE to be extra cautious when dating. Do you have any advice on how to weed out the good from the too good to be true?*

My advice to you, Brittany, is to first make sure that he really wants to get to know the real you. Make sure that he takes his time getting to know you and that he takes things slow. Remember that little gestures like calling just to say "hello" or sending flowers go a long way. It should feel like he is trying to get to know you, how your heart works, what your feelings are, and what your goals in life are.

If it doesn't feel this way, then move on. I firmly believe that the Good Lord put somebody on this Earth for each and every one of us to be happy with, to grow old with, and to have and raise children with.

There's definitely somebody out there for you, so keep your head up!

Magen asks:

> *What does a real honest cowboy look for?*

Magen, cowboy, plowboy, either way, most men look for somebody that is beautiful on the inside and out, has a strong set of moral values, respects themselves, and respects others.

I'm definitely looking for a woman that will be by my side through thick and thin, a woman that I love completely and a woman that I'm willing to do anything in the world for, someone that I can take care of and that can take care of me. I think most honest cowboys looking to settle down are looking for something similar.

Joana says:

> Younger [cowgirls] act like they have to act like "one of the boys" in the way they drink and curse. ... It saddens me to see the younger generation of ranch women/cowgirls forgetting that it's okay to look and behave like a well-polished lady. Perhaps your book could address the issue of ranch women/cowgirls being able to get the job done on the ranch while transforming into a lovely feminine lady when the work is finished for the day.

I think that most men that are looking to settle down are looking for someone that can act like a lady and be respectful of themselves. All the drinking and the partying is something that is out the window for a man like me that's looking for somebody to spend the rest of his life with. Seeing a woman carrying on in that way sends nothing but the wrong signals.

It's about having class if you want to attract a classy man. If you act like trash, you'll attract trash.

If you're going to be with a cowboy, you have to be a little rugged, a little gritty, and have a little of a rough edge to you, but that doesn't mean that you can't still be a lady. God made women different from men for a reason. It can be hard to balance the two sides, but remember that a man may like you for a little while if he sees you acting like one of the guys, but he ain't gonna fall in love with you.

Tamara asks:

> I have been married now for six years to my high school sweetheart. ... for over a year now he has stopped showing me any affection or even telling me he loves me. ... What is your thought on how to handle this?

Tamara, maybe your husband wants the love that he has given you for so long to come back to him. Maybe he feels like he's gone out of his way (as a man well should when he loves someone), but that now there's a void in his heart that he needs you to fill. It's probably time for you to go out of your way to do something for him, to stop by his work just to say "hi," or stop him in the morning on his way out and tell him you love him.

You have to remember that relationships are about working on things, and you have to put effort in and so does he. Maybe he feels like the relationship is just as one-sided as you do. Start by telling him you love him and showing him some affection to remind him of how you feel about each other.

Bubba Thompson's Cowboy Recipes

CORN PUDDING
1 can creamed corn
1 can whole kernel corn
1 stick butter (real butter)
1 box Jiffy cornmeal mix
8 oz. sour cream

Mix all ingredients together and place in baking pan; bake in oven on 350°. Cook until top is golden brown and firm.

HASH BROWN CASSEROLE
1 to 2 lb. bag hash browns
8 oz. sour cream
1/4 cup chopped onion
1 can cream of chicken soup
1 stick butter
Salt and pepper to taste
2 cups shredded cheddar cheese

Put thawed hash browns in large mixing bowl. Mix all other ingredients well and pour into potatoes. Stir well and put into large baking dish and bake at 350° for 45 to 50 minutes.

BUTTERMILK BISCUITS
2 ½ cups self-rising flour
2 teaspoons sugar
1/2 cup butter or shortening
3/4 to 1 cup buttermilk

Heat oven to 450°. Mix flour and sugar with fork. Cut in butter or shortening until mixture is crumbly. Stir in buttermilk slowly. When mixture leaves the sides of the bowl, take out the dough and knead it out on a lightly floured surface. Flatten it into a half-inch thickness. Take a flour-coated cutter and cut pieces and put in an ungreased pan 1 inch apart. Bake 10 to 12 minutes.

MEXICAN CORN DIP
8 oz. cream cheese
1 can Rotel tomatoes
1 can Mexicorn

Drain Mexicorn and put in sauce pan or pot and add a little bit of butter so the corn won't burn. Heat up till corn starts to sizzle, then remove from heat and put in mixing bowl. Drain the juice from the can of Rotel then add the tomatoes to the corn. Put the cream cheese in the mixing bowl. Mix all contents together. You can serve it warm or put it in the fridge and cool it down! It goes great with pita chips or tortilla chips!

BROCCOLI CASSEROLE
2 heads broccoli
2 cans cream of chicken soup
2 eggs
1 cup mayo
2 bags colby jack/cheddar cheese
Salt and pepper to taste

Chop broccoli and discard stem. Mix all contents in bowl, but leave half a bag of cheese to put on the top after cooking, or you can do it like Bubba and use a whole bag. Yeah, that's a lot of cheese, but heck! It sure is good!

APPLE DUMPLINGS
1 apple
1 tube crescent rolls
1/2 cup sugar
1/2 stick butter (real butter)
1/4 teaspoon cinnamon
1/2 cup Sprite

Peel apple, core, and cut into slices. Roll apple slices in rolls starting with wide end and place in a sprayed baking dish. On top of stove melt butter, sugar, and cinnamon on medium heat until it bubbles, then spoon it on top of the dumplings. Add the Sprite. Bake at 375° until golden brown.

COWBOY CHICKEN AND RICE
2 lbs. chicken thighs or chicken breasts
2 cans cream of mushroom soup
1 can cream of chicken soup
1 ½ cups rice

Wash chicken then place in baking dish. Mix rice and soups in bowl and pour over chicken. (I like to coat my chicken with my favorite seasoning then pour the mixture on top of the chicken.) Toss it in the oven on 400° and let it bake for an hour—but check it after 45 minutes 'cause some ovens are different.

ABOUT THE AUTHOR

Andrew Glassman is a television producer and former broadcast journalist.

Several of the television series he has created and executive produced through his company Glassman Media are relationship/dating programs including CMT's *Sweet Home Alabama*, and NBC's *Average Joe*.

Before producing television he was a news reporter for NBC television stations in his native Philadelphia, and later in New York City, and at CNBC where his reports were seen across NBC networks. He is the winner of multiple Associated Press awards for local reporting and a local Emmy for outstanding investigative journalism.

With passions including ice hockey and photography, Andrew currently resides in Los Angeles, where he is the proud uncle of two nieces Hannah, 13, and Cleo, 10.

He also sponsors a dirt track car at the Deep South Speedway in Loxley, Alabama, and owns a herd of cattle, and two horses on the open range in Alabama.

Made in the USA
Lexington, KY
27 February 2019